To Chris; I hope
Best wishes (Mel)

MASTER YOUR INNER CRITIC

RELEASE YOUR INNER WISDOM

practical steps to achieving
confidence, success and contentment

MELANIE GREENE
Chartered Occupational Psychologist
NLP Master Practitioner

summersdale

MASTER YOUR INNER CRITIC

Summersdale Publishers Ltd
46 West Street
Chichester
West Sussex
PO19 1RP
UK

www.summersdale.com

Printed and bound in Great Britain

ISBN: 1-84024-630-8
ISBN 13: 978-1-84024-630-8

Permissions

The author would like to thank the following for permission to reprint quotations from their work:

Dr Wayne W. Dyer, *Staying On The Path* (© 1995, 2004 Hay House Inc., Carlsbad, California).

Peter Karsten, *Be Great, Be You: A Little Book of Wisdom* (© 1999, The Chelsea Card Co., New Zealand).

Anne Dickson, *A Book Of Your Own* (1994, Quartet Books) with permission from Piatkus Books.

Daisaku Ikeda and Nichiren Daishonin with permission from Soka Gakkai, Tokyo.

SARK, *Living Juicy* (1994 Celestial Arts, Berkeley, California), *A Creative Companion* (1991 Celestial Arts, Berkeley, California), *Make Your Creative Dreams Real* (2004 Fireside, Simon & Schuster, New York).

The Hundred Verses of Advice by Dilgo Khyentse/Padampa Sangye Shambhala Publications ISBN# 1-59030-154-4.

Brian Keenan from *An Evil Cradling*

Barbara Cahill

Daphne Rose Kingma

About the Author

Melanie Greene is a chartered occupational psychologist. She works as a consultant, trainer and coach within both the private and public sectors, as well as running public workshops. Her work involves developing managers, assisting teams in communicating and working effectively together and helping individuals develop themselves both professionally and personally. In 1991 she set up her own consultancy, became a Buddhist and discovered NLP, all of which led her to where she is now. See www.grovelands.org.uk for more details.

She feels passionately about people being happy and fulfilling their full potential in life, whether through their work, their families, their hobbies, interests or voluntary work. With that in mind she writes a free monthly e-mail coaching newsletter, *Inspire*.

To my mum and dad for all their love and support over the years and for all the fun times together.

To my big brother, for keeping the Fun Child alive.

To Ali, the sister I never had – much better as a friend!

Contents

Introduction

'You're always a valuable, worthwhile human being, not because anybody else says so, not because you're successful, not because you make a lot of money, but because you decide to know it.'

Dr Wayne W. Dyer

Why I wrote this book

I hope this book will inspire you to take action to master and transform your inner critic, because I know that life without your inner critic is so much more fun, satisfying and relaxing.

In the past my inner critic was so strong that I spent most of my life in a state of anxiety, unhappiness and helplessness. Even when I was successful I did not enjoy my successes. However, by using the techniques in this book my life has been transformed, and that is what I want for you.

You deserve to be happy, fulfilled, to have the best and to enjoy all aspects of your life.

You don't have to put up with what your inner critic says and does to you – you can give it the boot and replace it with supportive, motivating messages. You can learn to manage your mood and thinking processes so that the inner critic cannot find a way in.

So many people suffer the effects of their own inner critics that it seemed selfish not to share my experiences and techniques with others. I hope that within these pages you will find inspiration, and techniques that will enable you to give your inner critic its marching orders. I look forward to hearing about your own experiences and stories.

How to use this book

This book will take you on a journey of self-discovery, guiding you through the process of recognising your inner critic and learning how to master it. Along the way you will explore methods for managing your mood, supporting yourself and drawing on your inner wisdom. You will learn how to put these ideas into action, both in terms of your own development and in your relationships with others. The techniques and exercises can be referred to at any time, so you can dip back into the book whenever you need reassurance or support in a particular area.

Find what works for you
There are many different ideas, techniques and models in this book, and my experience of running my 'Master Your Inner Critic, Release Your Inner Wisdom' workshops and coaching clients suggests that not all the ideas will suit everyone. Try each of the exercises and find which of them work best for you – by using them consistently and regularly you will be able to make changes for the better.

Create new positive habits
You might have been under the influence of your inner critic for many years, decades or a lifetime. You will have developed

habitual ways of thinking about yourself that are less than positive or downright destructive. Now is the chance to create new, more positive, constructive and supportive ways of thinking, feeling and behaving. Like developing any new habit or skill this will take practice – but with practice it will become second nature to think about yourself and life in a more positive way.

Use when you are under attack from your inner critic
There may be times when your inner critic is particularly harsh, loud or present in your life. You may have experienced a disappointment, or perhaps you've made a mistake and your inner critic is giving you a hard time about it. Perhaps you're facing a new challenge and your inner critic is undermining your confidence. At these times you can draw on the techniques in this book to counter your inner critic. When your inner critic strikes you can hit back to turn the situation around, to enable you to feel more positive, optimistic and satisfied.

My journey and my approach

Before I begin to explain the techniques and processes for mastering your inner critic, I'd like to tell you a little about my own background and the personal journey that has led me to write this book.

My experiences have developed me as a person and as a coach, trainer and consultant. Various approaches and philosophies that I have come into contact with have influenced my take on mastering the inner critic, and as you read this book you will be introduced to the different psychological models, Buddhist principles and other ideas that my clients, my friends and myself have found useful in mastering our inner critics and becoming happier and more satisfied in our lives. You don't have to be a psychologist or Buddhist to benefit from these ideas – I have attempted to distil these concepts into practical and, I hope, inspiring ideas for you to use.

You might want to think about your own background and the journey that has brought you to this point; the influences that have helped to create who you are and the roots of your inner critic.

My journey

I was born in 1963 into a Jewish family in south-west London. My great-grandparents on both sides had escaped to Britain from Russia at the end of the nineteenth century. My family is a very close one – probably as a result of continual ill health of family members that has brought us together over the years. I rejected Judaism and all forms of religion when I was 17 years old (the night of my dad's first heart attack), having questioned God and religion for a number of years.

I was a shy, under-confident and pretty unhappy child, teenager and twenty-something. I went to university to study psychology and I am sure that, like many people who study the subject, I was trying to figure myself out – the only problem was that a BSc and MSc did not seem to throw any light on my life and my unhappiness.

There was definitely a 'glass-is-half-empty' philosophy in my family and I applied this to all aspects of my life and the world around me. I focussed on my weaknesses, the ill health in the family, war, poverty and everything else that was wrong with the world – no wonder I felt so unhappy and anxious.

By the time I was in my second consultancy job, with a good salary and a company car, I was a home-owner, and was in a long-term relationship... and yet still deeply miserable, anxious and stressed. I decided to see a counsellor. The counselling helped me to understand a lot about how I had become the person I was, but it did not necessarily help me to become happier or less anxious.

A consultancy that I was working for took its employees through a kind of self-development process. One of the questions was,

'If a movie was made of your life, what would it be called?' As quick as anything I wrote: *Forever Searching*. This just about summed up myself and my life: I was forever searching for some meaning to the life I was living, which, to me, seemed totally pointless and miserable.

When a friend talked to me about Buddhism, I was intrigued, even though I was still very sceptical about any religion. The Buddhist concepts and philosophy really helped me to understand my life and the world in general. I liked the idea that the main aim of Buddhist practice was to become happy and help others to become happy. This struck me as a pretty good thing to aim for. For once I did not feel so helpless and hopeless.

The day after attending my first Buddhist meeting, I was made redundant. A few months later, I established my own consultancy, Grovelands Associates. Although I was still not particularly confident, I was determined to go it alone. By then I had started to chant and in the intervening years I have undergone a lot of personal and professional development. This development process has led me to learn how to master my inner critic; I often created my own techniques based on the ideas I had heard about. Over the years I could see the positive impact this was having on me, so I started to share some of the ideas with my clients. Now, I want to share my ideas with a wider audience through this book.

Your journey

Q. What have been the significant moments in your life that have brought you to where you are today?

Q. What turning points have you experienced that have had profound effects on you and your life?

Part 1

Understanding Your Inner Critic

'My inner critics were and are ruthless, and there is almost no acceptance of accidents, mistakes or missteps.'

SARK

Part 1 will assist you in gaining a full picture of your inner critic: how strong it is, when and where it kicks in, and the impact it has on your life.

Whether you are only just becoming aware of the pervasive nature of your inner critic or have been conscious of it for a long time, this Part will help you to fully understand the implications of your inner critic in your day-to-day life.

What do we mean by the term 'inner critic'?

The inner critic is that little (or sometimes big) voice in your head that says negative things like:

'You're not good enough.'
'Why did/didn't you say/do X?'
'You're hopeless, useless, moody, etc.'
'Nobody will want to hire/marry/be friends with you.'

These critical messages that run through our heads have a profound effect on how we feel, what we do, how successful we are, or whether we enjoy the successes that we experience in our lives.

Some people are very aware of the messages and conversations that are going on in their heads. Others aren't – until you start talking to them about the inner critic and they realise that for years they have being saying negative things to themselves, making themselves feel dreadful.

Some people have other names for the inner critic – the inner gremlins, the internal demon and so on – but all of these terms refer to the dialogue that goes on within our heads. When that dialogue is dominated by the negative voice (inner critic) it can be demotivating, destroying our confidence and stopping us from either fulfilling our potential or enjoying our lives.

Are you a glass-is-half-empty or glass-is-half-full person?

If you were presented with half a glass of milk, would you describe the glass as being half-empty or half-full? Of course, both answers are right in their way: it's a matter of perspective. The example makes a good analogy for people's approach to life in general: those who take the 'half-full' approach tend to appreciate the good things in their lives and the successes that they have. Those who come down on the 'half-empty' side tend to be the sort of people who focus more on what is missing from their lives, what has gone wrong and what has not happened.

The inner critic will always take the view that the glass is half-empty. If you are a glass-is-half-empty person, you can change this by learning to master your inner critic, by appreciating the good things in life instead of focussing on what is missing or going wrong.

How strong is your inner critic?

The following self-assessment will help you to identify how strong your inner critic is and the hold that it has on your life. It will also help you to identify where you might want to focus your attention in order to make changes.

Think about your daily life...	Always	Some-times	Rarely	Never
When you look back at your day do you only focus on what went wrong?				
Do you find it difficult to list your achievements and strengths?				
Do you fail to celebrate your successes and reward yourself?				
Do you lose sleep worrying about what you have done, or not done?				
Do you often feel unhappy, demotivated or demoralised?				
Do you fail to take credit when people compliment or praise you on your success?				
Is it difficult to give others compliments?				

Think about your daily life...	Always	Some-times	Rarely	Never
Do you feel guilty when you say 'No' to someone?				
Do you feel guilty when you ask for your own needs to be met?				
Do you allow criticism to get you down and dwell on it for a long time afterwards?				
Do you feel under-confident in your own ability?				
Do you constantly find yourself pointing out little mistakes others make?				
Do you worry all the time that something will go wrong?				
Do you let small things get you down?				
Do you often have a sense of humour failure?				

Your responses

Look at where you have ticked 'Always' or 'Sometimes': these are the areas you should focus on as you read this book. You might also want to bear in mind the items where you have ticked 'Rarely', depending on the impact these situations have on your life.

You might like to go back to this questionnaire from time to time to see how you are progressing. Try taking the questionnaire again and see how your responses differ from the first time. However, make sure you don't let your inner critic beat you up about your speed of progress.

Aargh- a compliment... just as well I have got my 'Yes But's in place...

Life with and without your inner critic

Read the following two stories and decide which one relates to you and your life...

Living with an inner critic

Tom wakes up in the night worried about a conversation that he had with his son. He wonders why he reacted so badly to what his son was saying. He feels that he is a terrible dad and as he keeps on playing it over and over in his head he finds it difficult to get back to sleep.

In the morning Tom wakes up and lies in bed, feeling awful. The sleepless night has not set him in a good mood for the business meeting he has that morning. His inner critic now starts saying: 'You are never going to make it to managerial level, this meeting is bound to be a disaster, you're no good at handling challenging people.' This is compounded by the messages from the night before: 'Why couldn't you just keep quiet and listen? Why did you have to overreact? No wonder he doesn't want to open up to you.'

Tom drags himself out of bed, has an argument with his wife over breakfast ('Don't know why she stays with you,' says his inner critic), and off he goes to work. During the meeting he wants to speak up and challenge something that is being said, but of course his inner critic tells him not to: 'Nobody is going to listen to you as you're not commanding enough,' or 'Don't say too much as they'll think you're too big for your shoes.' Either way, Tom can't win.

On his way home Tom reflects on the last 24 hours and feels thoroughly miserable as it seems like a catalogue of disasters.

Living without an inner critic

Tom has just had a difficult conversation with his son. However, unlike in the past he was able to control his reactions to what his son was saying, he listened and asked questions to attempt to understand his son. Although they did not come to an agreement, Tom goes to bed feeling he has done his best and even celebrating the fact that he is changing his relationship with his son.

In the morning Tom wakes up and lies in bed, and thinks about his day ahead. He has an important business meeting that morning, and his inner wisdom reminds him that, with the changes he has been making both in and out of work, he is managerial material. He visualises how he might handle any challenging people in the meeting and how he is going to get his key points across. He realises that his experiences with his son show that he can do this successfully.

Tom bounds out of bed, ready to face the day. His wife is worried about their son and he is able to listen and support her over breakfast. He walks confidently into the meeting, asks questions to clarify what people are saying and when necessary challenges what is being said. His manager thanks him for his contribution to the meeting and Tom feels really positive about himself and his strengths.

On his way home Tom reflects on the last 24 hours, which were full of a number of challenges. He is pleased with how he has handled everything and knows that he can build on these successes.

What is your life like?

You might not have children, but the same scenario can be applied to all of our relationships with colleagues, family members or managers. Whatever the situation, our feelings and behaviour are influenced by our inner critic and our ability to manage the impact it has on our moods.

Think about the two stories and about your life:

Which story is most like your life?
Are there times when you fall into listening to your inner critic and beating yourself up?
Are there other times when you either ignore it or it is not there at all?
What aspects of how you react to events would you like to change?

Different scenarios and your inner critic

Your inner critic can come into play in many different kinds of situations. Here are a few that have been mentioned in my workshops:

- When applying for jobs or going for interviews.
- Family get-togethers: dealing with other people's expectations, values, moods.
- Speaking at important meetings – especially if there are more senior people present.
- Presentations to certain audiences or on certain subjects – thinking you have to know everything to be professional.
- When we've made a mistake (big or small) and feel terrible about it rather than learning from it and letting go.
- Preparing for and going on dates, or romantic moments with partners.
- Meeting your child's teachers.
- Comparing yourself to others.
- Preparing for an appraisal.
- When you are feeling down or ill – your inner critic does not allow you time to rest and recover or you feel bad about taking time out.

The list could go on and on as your inner critic has the potential to impact on how you think, feel and behave in any situation, whether it's a potentially fun, enjoyable situation or a potentially stressful one.

Your life before and after mastering your inner critic

Until about ten years ago, when I was in my early thirties, I was harangued by my inner critic for what I said and did, or what I didn't say and do – so I couldn't win either way! I was permanently in a state of low-level depression; my moods were at the mercy of what was happening in my environment. It was not a pleasant place to be.

Now I am able to appreciate my strengths and realistically analyse situations when things do not go to plan. I am able to celebrate my successes and learn from my mistakes. The benefits are a more relaxed Melanie, who is happy in herself and able to deal with things when they go wrong, most of the time without it affecting her mood.

Q. What is life like now with your inner critic?
Q. What are the negative effects of this on you?
Q. How do you imagine life will be without your inner critic?
Q. What will be the benefits to you?

Focus on the benefits of change

You will feel more motivated to continue changing if you focus on these benefits. This will help you if the old inner critic starts to fight back. The vision of the benefits that you will feel, see and hear in your life will help to spur you on. If bringing about this change seems difficult, Part 6: Moving to Action will help you to get going and to keep going until you have mastered your inner critic.

Where did your inner critic come from?

As you read this book you might notice that I don't place much emphasis on looking at where the inner critic comes from. Although discussing the origins of your inner critic might help you to understand it, it may not help you to manage it.

The critical voice within us develops when we are children and comes from the messages we hear from a variety of sources:

grown-ups around us, parents, teachers, siblings, peers and other significant people in our lives. As children, we tend to take the critical messages we hear from others as true and do not challenge them. As we grow up we replay these internal messages (which might be reinforced by external ones) again and again in our heads, until they become habitual ways of thinking.

One thing I realised is that what my inner critic says is far worse and stronger than anything I heard when I was growing up. Something that might have been said only once to us as a child is repeated again and again by our inner critic, thereby strengthening the negative message. It seems that as children we take these messages to heart and are not able to rationalise them. As adults our inner child continues to react in the same way to these messages. However, as adults we can now respond differently, as this book sets out to demonstrate.

If you have not already identified where your inner critic comes from and want to explore this further, it is advisable to do so with the support of a counsellor, coach or trusted friend.

Blaming others versus taking responsibility

For me it has never been a case of blaming anyone for what goes on inside my head and my life. Of course I am a product of nature, nurture and, from a Buddhist perspective, my karma. Those people in my life who have influenced my thinking – my parents, teachers and other significant adults I grew up with – are also products of nature and nurture.

If you want to explore the past, think about your own life: your upbringing, the different influences on your early life. How have they shaped you? What positive and negative influences have they had? Also think about the influences your parents or other significant people were subjected to in their own lives. This will help you to understand the fears and concerns that might have affected the way they communicated with you.

In order to master your inner critic, you'll need to explore how you react to events now and change the patterns of thinking and behaving that were laid down in the past.

Let go of the past and create a bright new future

Shakyamuni Buddha said:

'If you want to understand the causes that existed in the past, look at the results as they are manifested in the present. And if you want to understand what results will be manifested in the future, look at the causes that exist in the present.'

Whatever your origins, the only thing you can do now is work on the present to create a brighter and happier future, by changing the way you think, feel and behave. Rather than dwelling on how you got to where you are and what created your inner critic, focus on what actions you can take today to create a wiser and happier you. By starting to use the ideas in this book you are making causes that will be manifested in positive ways in the very near future.

What does your inner critic look, sound and feel like?

One of the exercises in the 'Master Your Inner Critic, Release Your Inner Wisdom' workshop is to draw or make a collage of what your inner critic looks, sounds and feels like.

When I was piloting the workshop and introduced this exercise one participant immediately said, 'My inner critic says I can't draw,' and, not surprisingly, he has not been the last participant to say that! I suggested that he take a walk outside and see what he found that might relate to his inner critic. One of the things he came back with was a big stick – although it did not represent the 'big stick to beat himself up with' that many of us in the workshop had first thought.

I now provide lots of words and pictures cut from magazines for people to use as well as coloured pens to draw or scribble whatever comes to mind.

Make sure you have some time and space to focus on this exercise. People usually take about 10–20 minutes to complete it. Just draw (use words, symbols, pictures) or make a collage of the first thing that comes into your head when you think about what your inner critic looks, sounds and feels like.

Everyone's picture is unique, but here are some examples that participants have created:

- A drawing of themselves squashed under rocks with lots of 'shoulds' around them in speech bubbles, but with a door through a wall to their hopes and dreams on the other side.
- A dragon (they appear quite a lot).
- A room containing a filing cabinet full of 'shoulds' and 'to dos'.
- A sunny sky above, but a cloud over themselves (again quite a common image).

What to do next?

For some people just being able to manifest their inner critic starts to make it feel more manageable. One person decided to burn their picture when they got home to symbolically get rid of their inner critic. Others go back to their drawings and collages as they progress through the process of mastering their inner critic, often making changes to take the sting out of it.

Getting it out in the open is the first step on the road to mastering it. When you move onto Part 3 you will learn about a range of techniques to assist you in the process of transforming and taking the sting out of your inner critic.

The impact of your inner critic on your life

I was with a client, who worked as an operations director, and mentioned that I was writing a book. He asked me what the book was about. I wondered what he would make of the topic. When I told him, he said: 'Oh yes, I'm always focussing on what I do wrong or I don't get done, and I don't look at all the things that go well.' He then went on to say how this impacts on how he manages others. This made me think how our inner critic influences the many roles we play in our lives, as a:

Parent
Child
Sibling
Colleague, team member or manager
Friend

Whatever roles we play in life our inner critic will probably impact on how we behave in those roles and communicate with those around us.

You as a parent
This is applicable whatever the age of your children: 2, 10, 14, 20, 40, 50 – you still continue to be a parent. Your inner critic might affect you as a parent in a number of ways:

- You maybe overly critical of your children, perhaps setting excessively high standards for them.
- You may only focus on what they do wrong, rather than congratulating, praising and thanking them for what they

do well, whether it's tidying their room, coming third at long-distance running or getting a promotion.

- You may feel that you are not a good enough mum or dad – because you have overly high standards for yourself and you only focus on what you don't do or what goes wrong.

You as a child

Everything that is said above can be equally applied to us as children and our relationship with our parents. Does our inner critic lead us to:

- Set unrealistic expectations of our relationship with our parents?
- Focus on what they don't do for us and the things that go wrong?
- Fail to notice what they do and the good times we have with them?
- Not celebrate their successes in life?
- End up controlling or disempowering them as they get older (the inner critic is about control, not just of ourselves but of others around us)?

It is a challenge to find the right way of interacting with our parents and not allow our inner critic to interfere with this. The inner critic wants everything to be perfect and believes it knows what is right for ourselves and others. This can result in different types of controlling behaviour based on our inner critic's judgements. This could be something as simple as sorting through your mother's kitchen shelves and throwing out all the out-of-date cans: you might think you are being helpful, but in fact it is quite controlling. Or it could be about criticising them for their choices in life, how they wish to spend their time and money.

You as a sibling

Sibling relationships can be tricky and research shows that they can have just as powerful an impact on our development as our parents do. Many sibling relationships do not mature to a point of mutual respect and acknowledgement of differences, and they too can fall foul of our inner critic:

- Like everyone else our siblings can be judged harshly against our high expectations.
- Our inner critic may think they are cleverer, better-looking, funnier, happier, and generally more successful than us, leading us to judge ourselves unfairly against our siblings – which can also undermine our relationships with them.
- We can end up criticising their lifestyles, choices, the way they bring up their children. Whether this is overt or not it will affect the quality of the relationships we have with our siblings.
- Other family members can make comparisons between siblings. Do we act out the labels people give us: the funny one, the clever one, the pretty one? The inner critic will have a field day with these labels if we take them on board, telling us we are not as funny, serious, clever or pretty as our siblings.

You as a colleague, team member or manager

A colleague, team member or manager who has a strong inner critic and a glass-half-empty attitude might only focus on what goes wrong, on other people's weaknesses, on the problems – all of which leads to a demoralising and dissatisfying work environment.

Our inner critic can impact on working relationships in a number of ways:

- It can spark off critical reactions to what our colleagues or team members do, leading to unproductive if not downright destructive ways of interacting with others.
- Our perfectionist streak can also lead to intolerance of people doing things in a different way from us.
- Our inner critic might censure our ideas and creativity before we can share them with others, which will adversely affect our image at work and mean the organisation misses out on what we have to contribute in terms of ideas.
- When things go well either for ourselves or our work team, the glass-half-empty attitude can be a downer for everyone else if we fail to celebrate the success and only point out what could have been done better or still needs to be done.
- A strong inner critic can stop us from being able to relax at work and have a laugh with our colleagues.
- Unfairly comparing ourselves to our peers can impede our own development and lead to feelings of inferiority and dissatisfaction – it might even stop us from going for promotions or seeking better employment elsewhere.
- Our criticism of ourselves can lead us to feel unhappy and demotivated which can undermine our relationships with others.
- You may only focus on what others do wrong, rather than congratulating, praising and thanking them for what they do well.
- You may feel that you are not a good enough colleague, team member, manager – because you have overly high standards for yourself and only focus on what you don't do, rather than all the things that you do and that go well.

You as a friend

From my experience with friends it is often the bits of them that differ from me which add something special to the friendship. However, the old inner critic needs to be managed so it does not:

- Unfairly judge our friends regarding the quality or quantity of time they spend with us.
- Set too-high expectations of the friendship, which neither we nor they can meet.
- Result in paranoia when our friends spend time with other people.
- Set us up to compare ourselves unfairly to our friends and what they have achieved in their lives.
- Pass judgement on how they live their lives and the decisions they make (the inner critic is quick to say 'I told you so' when things do not turn out right).
- Lead to fear about being open about your mistakes and weaknesses (in case our friends are as critical as we are!)

Change yourself – change your relationships

Working on and transforming your inner critic will have a profound effect on all the roles you play in life and your relationships with others. You will be able to:

- Appreciate others for their strengths and differences and what they bring to the relationship, whether in your family, at work or in a friendship.
- Have a sense of gratitude for the people in your life rather than focussing on what is missing in them.
- Accept others' weaknesses and mistakes.
- Have more fun and laughter in all your relationships.
- See other people as supporters, mentors and sources of inspiration.

Your inner critic can all too easily get in the way of you having fulfilling relationships with your family, colleagues and friends. By using the different techniques in this book you will see how your relationships start to change.

Summary
This Part has been about you gaining a clearer perspective on how your inner critic operates in your life; the impact it has on you and your relationships. In Part 2, we will explore the role of our inner wisdom in our lives. Inner wisdom is a great antidote to our inner critic, and it also gets stronger as we learn to master our inner critic.

'I am always with myself, and it is I who am my tormentor.'
Nikolai Gogol

Part 2

Releasing Your Inner Wisdom

'Nine-tenths of wisdom is being wise in time.'

Theodore Roosevelt

Do you feel that your inner wisdom is rarely glimpsed or totally overpowered by your inner critic? This Part explores what we mean by wisdom, what happens when we ignore it and what blocks us from tapping into it. It also introduces some techniques to assist you in tuning into your inner wisdom.

What is wisdom?

It is interesting that when I speak to people about 'Master Your Inner Critic, Release Your Inner Wisdom' many people ask me 'What is wisdom?' Perhaps because we consider it as a virtue or a trait that is only applicable to learned elders or sages, we might wonder what it has to do with us and whether it exists within us.

However, I happen to know a ten-year-old boy who comes out with such words of wisdom he usually leaves the adults in the room speechless! I also know much older people who seem to lack any wisdom whatsoever, especially in their ability to repeat the same old destructive habits over and over again.

Years ago I might also have questioned the existence of wisdom within most of us – especially if you look at some of our behaviour. In Buddhism, wisdom is seen as one of the four characteristics of the state of Buddhahood that Buddhists believe everyone possesses. What I have witnessed in myself and others is that once we start to master our inner critics, our inner wisdom comes to the fore. Later, in Part 3, where we look at listening to our whole self and not just our inner critic, you will see that you can also start to unmask your own inner wisdom.

How do you define wisdom?

Wisdom is defined as 'good sense or judgement', 'keen discernment' and 'deep understanding'. Let's face it: even though at times we might act foolishly, we have also from time to time exercised good judgement, good sense and understood things from a more profound perspective. For some this might be a fleeting experience, for others a more regular occurrence.

However, our inner critic is unlikely to admit that we are wise. In fact the messages over the years from the inner critic are more likely to say that we are foolish, silly, ill-informed, stupid and so forth. So even if our inner wisdom makes an appearance there is a chance that we just dismiss it or don't even recognise it; we're certainly not likely to trust it.

What is wisdom like?

When I tap into my inner wisdom and use it to decide on a course of action or to make a decision, I feel totally at one with myself. There is no guilt or worry about what I have decided; instead there is a sureness and certainty in myself.

Q. What is it like when you tap into your inner wisdom?
Q. How do you know that it is your inner wisdom?

Intuition

I think there is a link with intuition. You know those times when you instinctively know what to do in a situation, when you suddenly find the answer to a problem you have been wrestling with? We all have those moments of inspiration, but we can so easily dismiss them. A by-product of mastering your inner critic is that your inner wisdom will find a stronger voice and place in your life. The more you use it the stronger it will become and the easier it will be to tap into.

Are there particular times when our inner wisdom is crucial?

Obviously it is important to tap into and use our wisdom on a daily basis, but are there particular times in the past when it would have been useful to tap into your inner wisdom? What about the future: are there decisions to be made or challenges to be faced where your wisdom needs to be leading the way?

Examples might include:

- Having to make an important decision at work or at home.
- Juggling the pressures of life and prioritising the needs of yourself, your family, your work commitments.
- Dealing with a difficult interaction with someone at work or close to you.
- Dealing with conflicting demands from different people.
- Attempting to balance your work, rest and playtime.

Whatever the situation it will be easier for you if you draw upon your inner wisdom. And that process will be easier if you practise tapping into your inner wisdom on a daily basis and not just in a crisis.

What happens if we ignore our inner wisdom?

If we ignore our inner wisdom we can end up feeling any or all of the following:

Overworked
Ill
Stressed
Tired
Low morale
Martyrdom
Depression

In fact, using your inner wisdom is the difference between stretching and straining yourself.

Recently, a friend who has a serious illness told me that, after having his fullest week back at work and a day out on the Saturday, he then collapsed on the Sunday and spent half the day in bed.

Does this sound familiar to you?

Holidays and weekends can either end up with us exhausted or ill, or still rushing around and having no down time to relax and refresh ourselves.

I believe that our ability to pace ourselves is linked to using our wisdom. Our inner critic can drive our behaviour with lots of 'shoulds' and 'musts' which keep us busy. During a session on the inner critic with a women's group, one woman said that from her Girl Guide days she learnt to 'always be prepared'. So that is how she has lived her life, always rushing around, doing excessive housework, making sure that everything is just so and prepared, just in case. Thankfully she did manage to laugh at herself and commented that she was not sure what she was prepared for, but prepared she was.

How will you benefit from listening to your inner wisdom?

Some of the benefits that others have found include:

- Knowing how to care for themselves when they are ill or going through a challenging time.
- Knowing when to ask for support or help.
- Feeling more sure and confident in their actions and about themselves.
- Knowing when they are wrong, and having the confidence and wisdom to spot mistakes, own up to them and learn from them.
- More energy, motivation, satisfaction and enjoyment of life.
- Being able to say 'No' or stop volunteering for everything.
- Stopping and resting before they get exhausted or ill.
- Knowing when to speak up (and when to stay silent) and knowing the right thing to say.

What blocks our inner wisdom?

If wisdom is always there then what stops it from coming through or stops us from experiencing it?

Have you ever been listening to an analogue radio station when interference has prevented you from receiving a clear signal? Listening to your inner wisdom can be a lot like that: you might sense the inner wisdom is around but find it hard to tune in and hear it clearly.

The interference in our heads often blocks out our inner wisdom. The noise from our inner critic or our fears can stop us from hearing and listening to our wisdom. If we have not learned to still our inner critic and inner fears, even if we have moments of insight we are either going to not hear them or dismiss them immediately.

What stops your inner wisdom?

Think back to times when you have had wise insights or your intuition has told you something – what has been your reaction, how have you handled this?

Times when you have followed your intuition or inner wisdom...

What happened? How did it feel?

Times when you have blocked your intuition or inner wisdom...

What stopped you? What was your inner critic or fearful self saying?

Radio Wisdom is always on air: it is just a matter of tuning into the signal. All the different activities and techniques outlined in this book will assist you in keeping the channel open and tuning into your inner wisdom:

Listening to your whole self (see Part 3)

This is essential for stilling the interference from the inner critic, fearful self and other bits of yourself. Once you master the art of doing this, your inner wisdom will become stronger.

Managing and changing your mood (see Part 4)
Learning how to manage your mood on a day-to-day basis will assist you in tapping into your inner wisdom. When we are in a negative mood we might have glimpses of wisdom but are unlikely to be in the mindset where we can take advantage of it.

Mastering your mind (see Part 4)
Dodgy logic and wonky thinking cloud the airwaves and make it difficult to hear and take on board our inner wisdom.

Creating empowering beliefs (see Part 4)
Limiting beliefs can undermine our inner wisdom, stop it from coming through or make us resist it when it does.

Q. What gets in the way of your wise radio signal?

Q. Are there particular times or situations when it's difficult to pick up the signal?

Q. Are there particular moods that make it difficult to pick it up?

Q. Or does fear or a lack of confidence and self-belief interfere?

Be your own agony aunt

Adversity is the mother of all invention
I 'invented' this technique very much from a place of adversity. I had a period when I was ill with a very bad asthmatic cough which went on for weeks despite lots of medical intervention, resulting in sleepless nights and me cracking a rib through coughing so much. During this period my mum, who suffers from a long-term illness,

also took a turn for the worse. Because of all this, I had to cancel a much needed trip to Venice – definitely a recipe for losing your perspective and forgetting your inner wisdom. There was one particular occasion where I needed to tap into my wisdom and I came up with a new way of doing this.

Dear Agony Aunt

I had just bought a new magazine that had come out called *Psychologies* and it actually starts with an agony column, rather than tucking it away on the back pages. I was in the situation where I was starting to get a bit better healthwise, and wanted to go to a Buddhist meeting that night as I had not been to one for a month and thought it would inspire me. But I was in a quandary about this. So I thought, what if I was writing to an agony aunt? What would she write back? This is what I wrote in my journal:

Dear Aunty Wise One,
I have been ill for five weeks with an asthmatic cough. I worked the first week, supported my mum the second one, got worse, rested, cracked a rib and then rested some more. I'm still not 100 per cent well – ignoring my rib, which is hard to do, I'd say I'm 75 per cent better, still occasionally coughing, but more today and being sick with it. I'm having problems resting and pacing myself. I want to get back to things and get on with my life. For example there is this Buddhist meeting I want to go to tonight, but I am not sure if I should go. Is it my wisdom or negativity that is stopping me going? What should I do?

And this was the reply from my own wise inner agony aunt:

Dear Melanie,
You have to remember to take time to recover from such a long illness and you now have your rib to heal as well. I think

you need to develop your patience and allow yourself time to recover. Listen to your wise self. Ignore your inner critic. You know you want to get back to things, but you need to pace yourself. Perhaps for today complete rest is needed. You are not someone who skives – don't allow any messages from your inner critic to convince you otherwise. Rest. Eat well. Be wise, chant to increase your life force and your wisdom.

With such words of wisdom I felt perfectly at peace with what I needed to do and the old inner critic did not get a look in.

How to get the most out of the agony aunt process

Like an agony aunt column in a magazine, this is written anonymously, so you can be open and frank about what is going on – nobody else is going to see it. This frankness in itself can be quite cathartic as you speak about your hidden fears, angst and pain. Writing your problem down, being able to read it rather than it going round and round in your head, can help you to step back from the issue and gain a different perspective on it. The reply from the agony aunt is likely to be more objective and rational than your internal view on the issue.

If you are uncertain about how to write from the agony aunt perspective, perhaps step into a good friend's shoes and write what they might say to you if they were an agony aunt. Or think about agony aunts you have read and respect – are they down to earth, frank, supportive or even provocative? Write from their perspective.

Q. In the past, when would it have been useful to write to your agony aunt?

Q. Are there situations coming up when the perspective of an agony aunt could be useful?

Developing your inner wisdom

In time, as your inner wisdom strengthens, it will become even easier to tap into your very own agony aunt. You will be surprised what your wise self has to say when you start listening to it rather than your inner critic, and you will start to benefit from your own inner wisdom.

The wisdom of mentors

So many times things that have loomed big and ugly in my head have seemed so much more manageable when talked through with a friend, coach, counsellor or mentor.

Even if you do become your own best friend (see Part 5) there are times when bouncing ideas off other people or just hearing what you are thinking out loud helps you to work things out for yourself.

Most of us have an inner critic, but we do not necessarily have a mentor!

Some people are lucky and grow up with someone who acts as an informal mentor in life. It might be a teacher, a neighbour or a relative who sees and accepts you for who you really are. They are non-judgemental, support you in your dreams, and do not write you off when you are less than perfect. For those who have had these mentors in early life, the positive impact can be felt throughout the rest of their lives.

Others acquire a mentor later in life. They might be provided with a mentor through their work, as more and more organisations use mentors, formally or informally, to support staff. In fact, many schools are setting up schemes where business people mentor students or teachers. In other cases, a mentor simply appears in your life or someone starts taking on the role without anyone labelling it as such.

What do we mean by a mentor?

A good mentor is someone who helps you to tap into your own wisdom, releasing your own potential. They can be a great counter force to your inner critic, helping you to see the folly of what your inner critic is saying.

Mentors for different parts of your life

Do you have a mentor? Would it help you to have a mentor in your life – a wise and trusted advisor? Mentors can be used in different ways and for different purposes. Some people have different mentors for different things.

What areas of your life do you want/need a mentor in?	Who could be your mentor?
Work/career	
Relationships	
Finances	
Parenting	
Health/Fitness	
Other	

Hidden mentors

Sometimes we might not be aware of someone being a mentor to us until we stop and think about it. It was only during a particularly tough time in my business that I realised that my dad was being an unofficial mentor to me. He used to run his own consultancy for many decades, spanning times of prosperity and times of recession, with many different highs and lows. His comments and his experiences of surviving the hard times encouraged and motivated me to carry on.

Is there someone in your life who you have not realised is playing this role? How can you make the most of them?

Wise words from virtual mentors

Even if you don't have an actual mentor or if you cannot contact them when you need to at a particularly challenging time, there is an exercise that can help you to tap into a mentor's wisdom. Virtual mentors are people who you call upon in your mind, rather than in reality. They could be dead or alive, fictional or real, mythical, historical, known to you or famous. You could even have an animal as a virtual mentor, for example drawing on the wisdom of a courageous lion or wise owl.

The following exercise works well if you have a decision to make or are facing a difficult problem. You can do this exercise in your head or on paper, but my clients and I find it works best if you move around, imagining that you are physically stepping into each of the mentors' shoes. You will need a private space to do this and enough room to step around into their shoes:

Step 1
Think about the issue or question you are facing.

Step 2
Think of three 'virtual mentors' whose wise words you would value hearing about this particular issue.

Step 3
Stand in your own shoes and look at your three virtual mentors standing opposite you.

Step 4
Take one of the mentors and step forward into their shoes. As you stand in their shoes, imagine you are them. From their perspective look at 'you' back where you were first standing. From their shoes give yourself some words of wisdom,

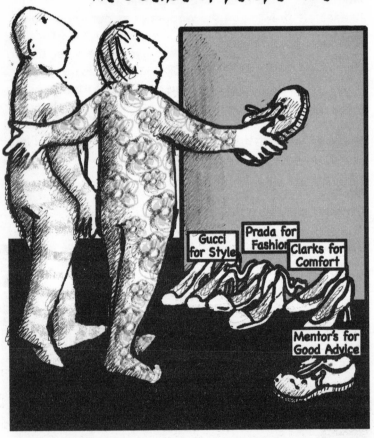

encouragement, support and/or inspiration. You can say the words out loud or just think them – the former is usually more effective.

Step 5
Step back into your shoes and spend a couple of minutes taking on board these wise words.

Step 6
Do steps 4 and 5 again with each of the other two mentors.

Step 7
When you are back in your own shoes, take on board the wise words from all three of your mentors. Then look up and visualise yourself acting on these wise words (see Part 4 on Visualising Success to help you with this process).

Virtual mentors and your inner wisdom
Even though during this exercise you are imagining what your virtual mentors would say to you, the wise words are actually coming from within you. By stepping outside of yourself and your problem you are able to gain a different perspective and tap into your own inner wisdom.

Q. When might you use this exercise for yourself?
Q. Are there decisions or situations you are grappling with now that would benefit from the use of your virtual mentors?
Q. Who might your virtual mentors be?
Q. What would they say to you?

Examples of when people have used the virtual mentors exercise:

- Making a decision about a career move.
- Balancing their own and other people's needs.
- Working out how to tackle a project with a tight deadline.
- When recovering from a long illness, wanting to throw themselves back into life, but needing to pace themselves.

A client had a tricky decision to make about work, whether to stay full-time or go part-time and have more time with their family. They were worried about the impact it might have on their career in the long term. This is what their virtual mentors said:

- (A friend) You are respected in your profession, you are passionate about your work and you will make it work even if you are working part-time.
- (Dalai Lama) Trust that whatever you choose to do you will make it work and be successful in it.
- (SARK) Look after the little child in you that is fearful about this change. Listen to her fears, rather than ignore them, and help her to deal with them.

This spurred her on to take the action to go part-time, which her employers supported, and so it was a win-win situation for all concerned.

The courage of a mentor

There can be times when we feel we are lacking in certain qualities, especially as our inner critic can tell us over and over again that we are not wise, courageous, funny and so on. To remind yourself of your inner qualities and tap into them, think of mentors virtual or real in terms of particular characteristics that they have and can offer you:

Q. Which real or virtual mentor could provide you with courage, compassion, wisdom, creativity or another quality you need?

Debriefing using your wisdom

Using our inner wisdom in all our day-to-day living is important, but one facet where our inner critic can run riot is debriefing ourselves after an event or an experience. Our inner critic takes over, spotting all the things that went wrong, undermining our confidence in ourselves and about the future, when this is actually the time to use our wisdom to reflect on what has happened and our successes, as well as learning from our mistakes.

Being able to debrief ourselves realistically and constructively is essential if we are going to achieve a sense of satisfaction and contentment in our lives and learn what we can from our past actions in order to grow and develop as people.

If we bring our inner wisdom into play when we review and debrief we are more likely to learn from a situation and celebrate our achievements. The questions below can assist you in realistically, constructively and wisely debriefing yourself.

What happened?
Think through or write down a non-judgemental, logical description of the situation. This will help you to gain a sense of perspective on what happened.

What went well? What were you particularly pleased with?
It is important to counter the inner critic by answering these questions and it might take practice for you to be able to identify and/or acknowledge what went well. Your inner critic might be saying 'Yes, but…' If it does, ignore it and carry on listing at least five things you did well. This can include how you redeemed situations that were going wrong!

What would you do the same another time?
I usually find that, even in situations when things did not turn out as planned or that were challenging, about 95 per cent of what I did I would do the same in another situation.

What would you do differently?
It is the five per cent that I would change that is likely to make the difference next time. Ask yourself, 'What is the difference that would make the difference?' It may be about how you would prepare yourself, manage your mood or control your reactions, all of which can impact on your behaviour.

What do you think someone else would have done in your shoes?
You might think about a colleague, friend or mentor (virtual or real). How would they have approached the situation? What would they have said and done? Obviously we all have different personalities and styles but we can learn from each other. It might be just one or two things from their approach that could make the difference.

What words of advice can you give yourself from either your own wise self, or from a respected wise mentor (real or virtual) to assist you in moving forward?
These might be words of advice, encouragement or to boost your confidence. This is about ending on a positive note to assist you in moving on and being optimistic about the future.

Learning from the past and in the future

It is important that we do learn from past experiences so that we do not repeat the mistakes. Therefore there might be situations where you would find it useful to go back and debrief using your wisdom.

Q. In which past situations would it have been helpful to wisely debrief?

Q. What situations are coming up where it would help to debrief using your wisdom?

Summary

I hope that by now you will be getting a sense of how you can tune into your inner wisdom and are starting to see how it can manifest itself in your life. The next Part moves onto techniques for mastering your inner critic which will further assist you in releasing your inner wisdom.

'Along the way to knowledge,
Many things are accumulated.
Along the way to wisdom,
Many things are discarded.'
Tao Te Ching

Part 3

Mastering Your Inner Critic

'The greatest discovery of my generation is that a human being can alter his life by altering his mind.'

William James

This Part provides you with a range of exercises and techniques for you to use to get to grips with your inner critic and start to master it. There are five sections:

Changing the message
A very effective way of mastering your inner critic is to realise that you can take control over the critical messages and take the sting out of the inner critic's tail.

Listening to yourself
As the inner critic usually shouts the loudest and our inner wisdom does not get heard it is important to start listening to your whole self. By learning how to listen to the different parts of ourselves we can start to get a more balanced view of life. Acknowledging our emotions and starting to listen to ourselves compassionately will act as an antidote to the inner critic.

Do less, be realistic

For most of your life you have probably been labouring under the tyranny of perfectionism, taking on too much, feeling guilty about what you don't do and failing to say no even if you are at breaking point. This section will assist you in being more realistic about the goals you set yourself or the 'To Do Lists' you draw up, and may even result in you doing less!

Fun, frolics and celebrations

Once you have changed the message, listened to yourself, are doing less and supporting yourself, there will be time and energy for fun and frolics. This is about encouraging you to celebrate your successes and have more fun in your life.

Changing the message

One of the ways in which you can master your inner critic is to 'change the message' that the inner critic is communicating to you. This can be done by playing around with what the inner critic looks and sounds like, as well as reframing its messages to reduce their impact on you.

Taking the sting out of the critic

There are lots of different ways of challenging, changing or minimising the effects of your inner critic. One way is to transform what is happening inside your head, by changing the voices and pictures that occur when your inner critic kicks in. By making small changes to the voice or pictures inside your head you can take the sting out of the inner critic and reduce or eliminate its impact on you.

Change the voice

One technique that works well for some people is playing around with the tone, speed or pitch of the inner critic's 'voice'. By doing this you are taking control of the inner critic and reducing its status: if you make it sound foolish, it will be much harder to take seriously.

You can do lots of things to change the 'voice' of your inner critic to make it sound less domineering or critical. Practise using some of the following ideas:

- A cartoon voice (squeaky, very fast or very slow).
- A whisper that you can barely hear.
- A distant voice that can't be heard because it is so far away from you.
- A feeble, weedy or very passive voice.
- Someone with hiccups (which will make it hard to hear what they say, or to take them seriously).
- A recent participant on a workshop decided to turn her inner critic into the voice of a humorous character from her favourite film, so that it would make her laugh when she heard it.

If the voice of your inner critic is usually female or male, switch it around. Play around with the tone and pitch of the voice – making it very high pitched or low can again make it difficult to take seriously.

Change the pictures

In Part 1, we dealt with the technique of visualising your inner critic by drawing a picture or making a collage to show what they look like. You might also have other images in your head associated with your inner critic: perhaps there is a certain situation in your life that makes you picture a dark, scary scenario, which is likely to make you feel anxious, under-confident and unhappy.

Create your own pictures

You can change any negative images so that they become positive and empowering. To help you to do this you need to visualise your inner critic. To assist you in this process you first need to look up to roughly where the wall meets the ceiling in a normal-sized room. When we look in different places (up, down, sideways) we access different parts of our brain, which influence how we feel and process information. When we look up we access our visual cortex and this enables us to visualise things more easily (for more about the visualisation process see 'Viualising success', Part 4). The great thing about this technique is that you can direct your own movie… play around until you are happy with what you see and hear.

Dress up your inner critic

This is a very effective way of taking the sting out of the inner critic. Try imagining your inner critic in a clown outfit, or other funny outfits – the sillier the better. One participant who drew her inner critic as a dragon dressed it up in a tutu with pom-poms. He suddenly looked silly, rather than scary, and his power immediately dissipated.

Change the size and perspective

Make the inner critic or negative image very small or very far away from you. The distance or reduction in size will make the threat less immediate and therefore easier to cope with.

Change the colour and contrast

If it is a colour picture, make it black and white, or maybe even like one of those old-fashioned movies, that are rather stilted and unintentionally comic. Adjust the contrast, making it lighter or darker, until you can't see the picture anymore.

Be dramatic and creative

Make the picture into a Laurel and Hardy or Superman movie, a children's cartoon or a period drama.

Remember you are in control

Part 4: Managing Your Mood has more ideas and techniques on how to master your mind and thereby manage your mood. It is about remembering that you have a choice: rather than letting your inner critic drive you to distraction and make you feel unhappy, demotivated or under-confident, you can make changes that will take the sting out of them.

Choose the right frame

Have you noticed how different a picture looks when its frame is changed? Any framer will tell you that the frame can make or ruin a picture. Choosing the right frame for the pictures in your head is about how you choose to look at something. It could be said that it is about what 'spin' you put on something, but it is far more positive than that. What often happens is that the 'frame' we choose for our life or particular situations is influenced by our inner critic, which tends to have a negative impact on how we view events and ourselves.

When you learn to spot unhelpful 'frames' and are able to make a positive change to how you frame or view them, you are likely to feel more positive, have more energy, feel lighter, more motivated and satisfied with life – so it is worth persevering until you have mastered the art of reframing.

Reframing your inner critic's thoughts and words

When you find yourself about to think or say negative, self-defeating statements, think about another way of framing what you are thinking and talking about that will be more empowering and motivating.

Statement or thought	Reframe
'I'm hopeless at having relationships.'	'I really need to learn from my experiences so that I can attract the right kind of person into my life.'
'Nothing ever goes right for me, I feel fed up and useless.'	'I am facing lots of challenges right now and it is tough, I need to look at what is going well and my strengths to build/draw on those.'
'I hate this task, it is going to be tedious.'	'There must be a way for me to make this task more interesting.'
'I'm never going to get this promotion, I'm just not up to the job.'	'Let's take a step back and look at the strengths I do have. Who could help me prepare for the interview?'
'You are pathetic, you never see anything through.' [said with the inner critic's scorn]	'Actually, that's not true. In the last few years I've passed my advanced driving test, completed an IT course and taken up tennis.'

Choose your words carefully

The words we use when we think and speak about a situation have a powerful impact on how we feel and behave, so we need to choose our words carefully. For example: do you face challenges, or problems? I find it useful to talk about the challenges that I am overcoming, rather than problems or difficulties I have to face. This might seem like semantics, but how we view things and the words we use to describe them will have either a positive or negative impact on our ability to deal with the situation in hand.

Change your outlook

Whether we have a 'glass-is-half-full' or 'half-empty' view of life affects everything in our lives. Do you look at what went wrong or what went well? Do you focus on what did not happen or what might happen in the future? Do you think about what you don't have in your life, rather than appreciate all the things you do have? These different ways of thinking again affect how happy and satisfied we are with our lives and the actions we end up taking. Many people feel that this is part of their personality and you are either an optimistic or pessimistic person. However, from my own experience and from working with clients I know it is possible to change the glass from being half-empty to being half-full.

Reframing the picture in your head

As well as changing the pictures in our head, we can change what we focus on when we look around us. If, when we think of something that has happened or that is going to take place in the future, we have negative images in our mind's eye, we can reframe it and see it in a more positive, empowering and motivating light. See Part 4 on 'Visualising success' for more assistance with doing this.

Start reframing today

If you have found this difficult to do in the past then start today. What negative statements from your inner critic would you like to reframe?

Q. What do you need to reframe?
Q. How can you reframe it?

'There is no such thing as a problem without a gift for you in its hands. You seek problems because you need their gifts.'

Richard Bach

Listening to yourself

We might have spent our whole life listening to our inner critic, but we probably have not spent much time listening to the other parts of ourselves. This section is designed to assist you in becoming better at listening to your whole self. By acknowledging our emotions, being compassionate towards ourselves rather than letting our inner critic kick us when we are down, we will have made great strides towards mastering our inner critic.

Conversations with your inner critic and inner wisdom

In daily life, if someone is constantly bullying us and undermining our confidence, the last thing we want to do is sit down and have a conversation with them. We might not want to listen to what they have to say and probably feel that there is no way they are going to listen to us. We can often feel the same about our inner critic. However, from my experience, if I ignore it for too long it just gets louder and more extreme in its views, and makes me feel even worse about myself.

There is a model that is used to help people understand how they interact with others called Transactional Analysis, or TA for short. This model can also be used to explore our inner dialogue, to find out not only what the inner critic is saying, but also what the other parts of you are thinking and feeling, the parts that usually don't have a say because the inner critic is so loud and strong.

The TA model shows that we have learned ways of communicating and reacting to events. We often end up habitually responding in a particular way. But once we understand this we can start to choose the appropriate mode for different situations.

According to the TA model, there are three modes that we learn to communicate from:

These are labels for learned ways of behaving. They are not

Parent mode	this can be: • Nurturing, caring or rescuing, overprotective or disempowering • Controlling, critical, overpowering
Adult mode	this always: • Is assertive, clearly communicating wants, needs and feelings • Aims for a win-win situation, does not play games • Listens to what the other person is saying • Respects their own and other people's rights • Manages their emotions and remains rational and calm • Takes responsibility for decisions, actions taken and mistakes
Child mode	this can be: • Fun-loving, happy and carefree, creative, energetic and enthusiastic • Adaptive, going along with social norms, customs, etc. • Fearful, anxious, rebellious, wilful, obstinate, sulky or manipulative (you tend to experience one of these negative sides of the Child mode more than the others).

the same as physically being a parent, an adult or child. We all have the capacity to behave in Parent, Adult or Child mode, and each one has its time and place. We don't have to be a parent to have an 'internal parent' within us. Also, although physically we might be adults we do not always behave like the Adult mode described in this model; in fact we can often fall into the Child mode. This is especially so when we face difficulties or conflict.

The following clarifies what the Parent, Adult and Child modes mean, and how they relate to us and our inner critic.

Parent mode

The Parent mode is within all of us, regardless of whether we are actually parents. It contains behaviours that we witnessed as a child in the grown-ups around us: our parents, teachers and other significant people. We thought that was how a grown-up acted, when what we often witnessed was parental behaviour, either nurturing or controlling.

Our inner critic is our internal Critical Parent replaying the negative, controlling messages that we picked up from the adults around us who were in Parent mode. For some people this is all they ever hear as it drowns out the Adult and Child voices within themselves.

On the other hand the internal Nurturing Parent cares for and supports us. For some people who have a strong inner critic the internal Nurturing Parent is almost non-existent. They do not know how to care for themselves, they only know how to criticise and undermine. So strengthening your Nurturing Parent is an important part of mastering your inner critic.

Child mode

Even though we are adults we still have the child inside us. There is the Fun Child, which is where our sense of enjoyment, humour and creativity comes from. Life would be very dry and boring without it. When we tap into our Fun Child it energises and refreshes us.

While running my workshops it is evident that that for many people with a strong inner critic their Fun Child does not get a look in; either they don't make time for fun, or the Fun Child has not been developed at all while they were growing up. If this rings a bell with you, see 'Releasing your Fun Child' later in this Part.

The Adaptive Child is that part of us that goes along with various social norms and conventions: we queue at bus stops; we are polite towards others. Our society is partly kept together by our Adaptive Child behaviour, as without it there could be anarchy. However, if someone has a very strong Adaptive Child they are likely to go along with what their inner critic says without questioning it. They might become passive in situations, not able to speak up for themselves or question things. Sometimes I see this during workshops: a few participants go into Adaptive Child mode, and they go along with everything that is asked, but never seem to be fully engaged. I would prefer to have an argumentative participant than an adaptive one any day, as they are engaged with the process and, if handled well, usually get more from it.

Those people with a strong Adaptive Child can find themselves kowtowing to their inner critic, believing that the inner critic knows best. They think that they 'must' behave in a certain way: they 'should' do X and Y in order to be a good child, parent, manager or colleague, rather than exploring who they really are and how they want to behave.

The other aspect of the Child mode are the negative reactions we have to situations. This can be the Fearful, Anxious, Rebellious, Wilful, Obstinate, Sulky or Manipulative Child which is left over from our own childhood and our habitual ways of behaving. You will find that you have a leaning towards one or other of these types of child. For example, I used to have a strong Fearful Child, but I don't really have a Rebellious or Sulky Child in me. In fact we weren't allowed to sulk in our family and I am still mystified by other people's sulky behaviour, especially when I hear that someone has been sulking for a whole week or two! A lot of my colleagues have a very strong Rebellious Child that can be triggered when they think you might becoming parental with them.

A recent participant on a workshop said that her Rebellious Child had a habit of reacting against her inner critic. If this happens with you and you do not tap into your inner wisdom, it can lead to destructive behaviour, where the Rebellious Child says 'I don't care what I "should" do, this is what I am going to do,' regardless of the consequences.

The Fearful Child can often get neglected as a strong inner critic will scoff at its fears. There can be other reasons why the Fearful Child gets ignored. For one client experiences from the past meant that they were frightened even to start listening to their Fearful Child, in case it got out of control. Fortunately, by doing the listening exercise on the next page they are able to start listening to their Fearful Child.

Q. Which Child mode do you think you most often fall into?
Q. What situations trigger this in you?

Adult mode

You might be forgiven for thinking that we are adults and therefore we all behave in Adult mode. However, if you look at the descriptions in the TA model table a few pages back you will see that this is not always true, especially when problems occur or we are in conflict with others. It is then that we often slip into either Parent or Child mode. Yet it is during these difficult times that we need to engage our Adult mode, step back and look at things in a more rational way.

Communicating with your internal parent, adult and child

We all have within us an internal Parent, Adult and Child, with their own views and emotions associated with different topics and situations. And like any family, some get their views across more strongly than others. For those of us with an inner critic it is usually their voice that is the loudest, while the others might not get a word in edgeways.

The following process is a technique that I use to listen to all of the different modes within me. It helps me to identify what is really going on for me in a particular situation and what I need to focus on. Using this process over a number of years has had a profound effect on how I react to and deal with challenges that I face. My clients also find the process very useful both in terms of mastering their inner critic and tapping into their inner wisdom.

There are two ways you can do this exercise:

- Write down what the different parts within you are saying.
- Physically move around and step into the Parent, Adult and Child modes, saying out loud or thinking through what each is saying.

I tend to turn to my journal and write down the conversation between the different modes that is running through my head. Here is an example from when I was experiencing some indecision about an impending trip to New Zealand:

Critical Parent

'Why do you feel you deserve six weeks off when others can't have it?'

'It is a lot of money to spend, you could give it to charity or put it towards a new house.'

'When are you ever going to get your book written?'

Nurturing Parent

'What a load of tosh – everyone deserves six weeks off, but they are often not brave enough to take it.'
'You give loads of money to charity.'
'You will complete the book by the end of summer.'

Fun Child

'Yippee, I can't wait! Six weeks of freedom, lots of new experiences and adventures. This is great!'

Fearful Child

'What if it rains the whole time?'
'What if I don't enjoy it as much as last time?'

Adult

'Everyone is happy for you to be doing this – even if some may be a bit envious.'
'You deserve this and have earned it after the year you have had.'
'You will enjoy it whatever the weather – and in six weeks the sun will also shine.'
'Do some work with your coach on what might help and hinder you in writing your book.'

Getting a clearer picture

Whenever I do this exercise I always feel clearer about what I need to do, happy about decisions I have made and more relaxed about life and myself. Some time ago I received an e-mail from a client that made me laugh. It went something like this: 'My Parent, Adult and Child just sat down at the kitchen table with a cup of tea and had an open and frank chat. And when I got up from the table I felt so much more motivated and energised.'

Key points to bear in mind when having your 'conversation':

- You can start with whatever mode seems most appropriate; however, as the inner critic always has so much to say it is often useful to let it go first. Then once it has spewed out all its criticisms the other modes can give you a different perspective on the situation. Also, the inner critic can have some valuable points to make, the problem is how these are presented: its tone of voice, stating things as fact with no room for discussion. This exercise means that you can discuss what the inner critic says rather than taking it at face value.

- If you are not used to listening to your Fearful Child, it is important you start: let it bring out all its fears and concerns. If you don't they will bubble away below the surface and impact on your mood and happiness anyway. So you might as well get them into the open and face your fears – bearing in mind your Nurturing Parent will help you to deal with them.

- Your Fun Child also needs to be heard, as with our inner critic life can become very staid and joyless. Your Fun Child is probably dying to come out and make suggestions as to how life could be lighter and more enjoyable.

- Do you have other parts of the Child mode that have something to say? Is your Rebellious Child gathering resources for a rebellion? Are you feeling sulky? What else is going on for you?

- If you are not used to nurturing and supporting yourself you might find that the Nurturing Parent is going to take time to be fully functioning. However, bring them in on any conversation and in time they will become stronger and have some words of wisdom on the situation you are facing.

- I often bring my Adult mode on last. Having allowed all the others to have their say, the Adult mode can step back and look at the situation in a more logical and rational way. It can then provide some words of wisdom based on what is right for all of you, allowing you to move on and better handle the situation that you are facing.

- If you have not done this kind of process before it will take practice for you to find a method that suits and supports you. The benefits of doing this are that you create a new way of thinking and approaching inner conflict. And the end result is feeling clearer, more focussed, more energised and motivated.

Changing the order of your conversation

You might want to do it in a different order and sometimes I change it around to suit what is going on for me at that moment. As you get used to using this process you will naturally know which order to go with to suit the situation or the mood that you are in. The other day, the Fun Child wanted to get in there first, then the Critical Parent and the Nurturing Parent. Over the years, I have realised that my 'wise self' is a combination of my Adult and Nurturing Parent. Therefore when I write things down nowadays I just refer to my Wise Self or Wise Melanie who always seems to know what to do.

When would it be useful to listen to the Parent, Adult or Child?

Some of the time our inner critic can create internal conflict where different parts of us appear to want to do different things, or think that different courses of action or decisions should be taken. This inner conflict can be about anything and can last a few minutes, to days, months and even years of conflict, indecision and unhappiness.

The following are examples of inner conflicts that I, and some of my clients, have experienced. Some are conflicts about future possibilities, while others are about past events:

Inner conflict before events:
- Whether to take a job which will mean more pay and perks, but is taking the person away from their dreams.
- Whether to become self-employed and give up the security of a job.
- Whether to spend time looking after a sick mother who is miles away or focus on your career.
- Whether to do a PhD or have a family.
- Whether to go to a party at the weekend or stay in and chill out.

Inner conflict after events:
- Why did you said X to Mr Big at the meeting?
- Why didn't you take the opportunity to take time out and travel when you were young?
- Why did you follow your father into the family business instead of following your dreams?

Internal conflicts or being at odds with yourself can lead to unhappiness, indecision and, if prolonged, can lead to tension, illness and depression.

Think about different situations when it would be useful to listen to the different parts of yourself. The following are situations where people have called on the different modes:

Nurturing Parent
When they were ill, tired, down, facing problems beyond their control; when they needed support and care, rather than criticism.

Adult
When they needed to step back and look at a situation in a more rational way, removing the emotional element.

Playful, Fun Child
When they were on holiday, having time out; when faced with difficult situations, especially ongoing ones, and in need of some fun to re-energise and motivate themselves.

Fearful Child
When something was stopping them from moving forward and they were not sure what it was – often underlying fears can be the cause of indecision and lack of progress.

Rebellious Child
If your behaviour seems to be self-destructive it might be useful to consult your Rebellious Child and find out what it is rebelling against.

Sulky Child
Are you sulking? Is there something that you have not dealt with directly or are avoiding?

In the above exercise I have not mentioned the Critical Parent, represented within us by the inner critic, as I feel from experience that whatever the inner critic has to say would probably come across better from either the Nurturing Parent or Adult modes. So although I suggest that you do listen to what your inner critic has to say, it's best not to call upon it on its own – make sure you listen to the other parts as well.

Compassionate listening to ourselves
We need to become skilled at this process of listening to ourselves and learn how to do it from our Nurturing Parent, with compassion for ourselves. Instead it is often at the times when we most need to listen to ourselves compassionately that we end up kicking ourselves.

If we are very lucky we have someone who will listen to us attentively and compassionately, without having to pay them to do so. However, there are times when others are not around and therefore being able to compassionately listen to yourself is important. I find it helpful to use my journal to think through things, to get my emotions out of my head and attempt to make sense of what is going on inside. Listening to my inner Parent, Adult and Child enables me to understand the different parts of myself that are often in conflict with each other.

Think of past situations when it would have been useful to have listened to yourself.

Q. What emotions did you need to acknowledge?

Q. What situations are coming up in the near future where it might be useful to listen to yourself?

Q. What emotions might you need to acknowledge?

Silencing the inner critic

I found myself in a situation recently that made me laugh. I realised that there was some internal conflict going on about a challenge I was facing. I listened to the different parts of me and when it got to my inner critic it said, 'I give up, I know that what I am about to say is a load of rubbish!' It seemed that my wise, nurturing self had won over in that situation – my inner critic did not have a leg to stand on.

There will already be conversations going on within you on a daily basis, but they are probably dominated by your inner critic. By using this process of listening to the other parts of yourself you will start to make these conversations overt and balanced, rather than a one-sided rant from your inner critic.

Acknowledge your emotions

I have a client who has a very strong inner critic and is continually beating herself up, giving herself a hard time about what she has not achieved and done. She actually has a responsible position in an international company. She is very conscientious in her role and has successfully moved from her homeland and created a life in the UK. But of course her inner critic does not acknowledge any of this and just berates her for not passing her driving test, not losing weight and many other things that she has supposedly not done or has failed at.

Denying how we feel

In my discussions with this client I was talking about the fact that our inner critic can stop us from feeling our real emotions. If we end up suppressing our emotions they can come out in other ways, as illnesses, depression, overeating, drinking too much or other addictions.

The inner critic tends to mock and ridicule us for our fears, anxieties, or insecurities. Your inner critic might say things like:

'Don't be so stupid, you can't be scared about X, you're an adult; you've done it before or nobody else reacts like you.'
'Grow up, pull yourself together.'
'You are pathetic to be scared of that.'
'You're such an angry person, but you never do anything about it.'
'You are always sulking and behaving badly when you don't get your own way.'

This constant berating is likely to suppress some if not all of our emotions. For me it led to many years of continually feeling anxious, unhappy, and even at times hopeless. For this client there is likely to be a link between her inner critic, her suppression of her feelings, her overeating and even her inability to pass her driving test. Instead of denying our emotions we need to listen and deal with them head on.

> **Q.** Are there emotions that you have been suppressing?
> **Q.** What does your inner critic say to you about this?
> **Q.** How does this affect your health and happiness?

As mentioned, my client had difficulty passing her driving test. The inner critic berated her for this, saying: 'You're an adult, this is something you should have achieved by now.' Before taking her test she was understandably very anxious, had difficulty sleeping and did not feel confident about herself and her ability. As you can imagine, this is not exactly a recipe for success!

Another client of mine was suppressing his anger about the lack of development and promotion at work, and was regularly getting headaches. His inner critic was telling him: 'You're pathetic. You keep on getting passed over but don't do anything about it.' He was fearful that if he said something he would explode. By learning to listen to his Fearful Child as well as his anger he was able to plan out a constructive way forward through talking to his manager about his career hopes and his desire for development.

Fearing our negative emotions

People can fear their negative emotions, especially if they have spent a lifetime ignoring or suppressing them. It can be frightening to feel these emotions. You might wonder how you will handle them: will it get out of control, will it be worse than suppressing them? All these feelings are understandable and need to be faced. I often hear people saying, 'If I start to cry I may not stop,' but so far I have never heard of anyone carrying on crying forever! When I first started to challenge this area of my life there were a lot of tears. And in time I learned that was entirely OK.

Often the tears or feelings of anger can be at ourselves, and what we have done to ourselves over the years. Maybe we realise that through our inner critic we have been so cruel to ourselves for so long that we have missed out on opportunities and held ourselves back from realising our dreams.

It's reassuring to know that, rather than stay stuck with this regret and anger, you can start afresh by fully acknowledging your emotions and learning to experience the highs as well as the lows in life.

Support yourself in this process
It is helpful to get support from either professionals (a coach or counsellor) or good friends who will be able to accept you for who you are, not belittle what you say or feel, and help to empower you through the process. Who could you turn to for support? Who would create a safe and constructive environment to discuss your emotions with?

No experience is wasted
Occasionally I have thought about how great it would have been if I tackled these issues in my teens. Maybe if I'd seen a counsellor or become a Buddhist when I was young I could have saved myself a lot of suffering. But without those experiences, I wouldn't have had anything to inspire me to write this book and try to help others to overcome their inner critic.

It's no coincidence that many people who take supportive roles have been through similar experiences to the people they are supporting. Whether they have been faced with depression, bereavement, addictions or rape, once they have worked through their own emotions connected to these experiences they are able to use them to help others.

So, rather than have regrets about the past, think about how you might use it in a positive way in your life. This might be by drawing on your own experience to support others. Alternatively, the fact that you have wrestled with these challenges in your life may have made you a more rounded and wiser person, which in turn will have a positive impact on how you approach other things in your life.

Suppressing good feelings

Strangely, our inner critic can also have a go at us when we feel good, which can result in us suppressing our good feelings as well. It can say things like:

'It won't last.'
'What have you got to be so happy about?'
'OK, but you still have not done X or achieved Y...'
'It will end in tears.'

Talk about a killjoy!

Once you have transformed your inner critic you will find that you are able to acknowledge all of your emotions, enjoy the good ones and learn to manage and cope with the negative ones. The part on Managing Your Moods will provide you with more ideas about how to recognise your emotional state and what to do to transform it when you are in a less than positive one.

Acknowledge your positive emotions

Delight, joy, satisfaction, calmness, happiness, passion, contentment, ecstasy... Think of a recent positive situation where your inner critic ended up ruining it for you.

> **Q.** What positive emotions are you missing out on because of your inner critic?
>
> **Q.** What does your inner critic tend to say to you when you start to experience these positive emotions?
>
> **Q.** What might your Fun Child, Nurturing Parent and Adult modes say to you to encourage you to relish your positive emotions?

Whenever you start to feel positive, watch out for the inner critic undermining you. Listen and revel in your positive moods.

Do less, be realistic

Our inner critic usually drives us on to do more and more, often resulting in overdoing, overload and feelings of being overwhelmed by life. This section explores the roots of our perfectionism, guilt and inability to be realistic and say no. It will provide you with some insights into your overdoing and enable you to start to set more realistic targets for yourself.

The tyranny of perfectionism

When I was younger I used to bite my nails and as a result they were very weak and wouldn't grow very long. A few years ago a friend commented on how long and wonderful my nails looked and I turned round and said: 'Yes, but look – this one is broken.' My friend replied: 'That sums you up, nine out of ten nails are perfect and you focussed on the one broken one!'

The incident has stuck in my mind as it graphically showed my 'glass-is-half-empty' tendency. We can often hide this negative tendency under the banner of perfectionism... but so far I've not met a happy perfectionist! Perfectionism means that we want everything to be correct, everything done, everything sorted before we can relax, feel a sense of satisfaction and enjoy ourselves. It is only by conquering the perfectionist tyrant that we can truly enjoy our successes.

The perfect life

I saw how much I had changed when I first fell ill with very bad allergies in 1998. I remember lying in bed one night, having cracked my ribs from coughing too much. It was after a five month stretch of being ill most nights, where I ended up unable to work (a difficult situation for a self-employed person). I lay there and thought: 'Well, it's not life-threatening, I have some savings, I have a wonderful family who love me, I have friends, I have a lovely home.' The old 'half-empty' me would have said, 'Here I am with no work, no relationship and really ill and I've cracked my rib!'

Perfection at work

In my work I used to find myself focussing on the one participant during a workshop who was negative or not appearing to make any changes and judge my success by them. Now I focus on the 99 per cent who are ready and willing to change, which results in me feeling more positive about the process, and gaining a sense of success at the end of the programme. Interestingly as my focus moved away from the 1 per cent who were negative, and as I responded to them in a different way, they often reacted to the process differently and became more positive.

I have cracked the tyranny of perfectionism, viewing my glass as half-full, and the difference in my sense of satisfaction, contentment and happiness is huge.

Getting a balanced view on your life

It is our inner critic that hounds us about being perfect and stops us from realistically reviewing our life, our work and our strengths. The following exercise will help you to start thinking about all the good things in your life and about yourself.

List all the good things that are happening in your life at the moment	List all the good things about yourself

As you work your way through this book, you may find you are able to come back to these lists and add to them.

For example, people say about their own life:

- My family are close and supportive.
- I have a comfortable home.
- I have a short commute to work.
- My children are doing well at school.

What people say about themselves can include:

- I'm determined to win through on a particular work issue.
- I'm courageous in tackling a difficult relationship.
- I have taken up new interests and hobbies.
- I have taken time to get fitter despite time constraints.

Realistic reviewing

When you review an event or period in your life, be sure to list the highs and lows, rather than just focussing on what is missing. Even if you are reviewing something you have found particularly tough, you may be pleasantly surprised to find that the highs outweigh the lows. However, without listing them, it is easy to focus on the negatives rather than the positives. The reason you need to list the lows as well as the highs is that it is important to acknowledge the challenges you are facing in life, along with any negative emotions that are associated with them. Then you are in a position to find ways to overcome and deal with them.

Think about the last month.

Q. What have been the highs?
Q. What have been the lows?
Q. What do you need to do to learn from the last month and move on?

Here's an example: a coaching client had many highs during the previous month, with new and satisfied customers. However, the main low was that he was not achieving a balanced life; he was not exercising enough and was feeling lethargic. By acknowledging the lack of progress in this area and taking a step back to look at how he structured his week he was able to identify where he needed to be more efficient, what things he could delegate and how he could create more time for exercise. He also found a swimming pool near to his work where he could go swimming before the working day started, thereby missing the traffic and getting some exercise.

Approximate perfection – breaking the tyranny of perfection

'The battle to keep up appearances unnecessarily, the mask – whatever name you give creeping perfectionism – robs us of our energies.'

Robin Worthington

Those of us who have high standards are probably already putting more time and effort into our jobs and relationships than many other people. Therefore, even if we appear to not meet the perfectionist standards of our inner critics and go for 'approximate perfection', we will still be giving more than enough attention to the task in hand.

It was my friend Peter who came up with this idea of 'approximate perfection', which is a much more realistic way of looking at life. In fact we can only ever achieve 'approximate perfection', as the high standards of complete perfection are, thankfully, beyond most if not all of us.

Being good enough

Many years ago while travelling in Canada I came across a very innovative and creative writer called SARK, and her books have been a constant source of inspiration to me. She often talks about:

Being enough
Having enough
Doing enough

It took me a long time to really understand that I was enough just as I am, as a human being. Most of us think that we are not enough as we are, we think that there are skills or qualities that are lacking and we need to be more than who we are. Starting from the notion that we 'are enough' is much more motivating. Yes, we might wish to develop ourselves, but this does not mean that we are wanting in the first place. The same is true for what we have. Obviously, there are huge inequalities in people's lives and what they have. However, the majority of people reading this will have enough to survive, even if there are things we desire. In terms of what we do, fuelled by our inner critic we usually do more than enough in work, in our families and in our communities, yet we still think we need to do more.

Think about yourself now – you are good enough just as you are now – with all your great strengths, human flaws, courage, fears, achievements and unfinished projects.

Q. What happens when you think about that?
Q. How does it make you feel?
Q. Do you believe it?
Q. What is your inner critic's response?

If your inner critic is saying 'No way are you good enough, what about the mistake that you made the other day, what about your fears, insecurities, unfinished business…?' then you might want to turn to the next section on 'Being realistic'.

Being realistic

Do you find that you set yourself unrealistic goals? When planning your diary do you think it will be alright until you get to a particular week, then find yourself asking 'What was I thinking, why did I

squeeze so much in?' With a strong inner critic we can all fall foul of this, but by eliciting our inner wisdom or wise mentor we can either avoid this or find our way out of such situations.

One year I had set myself the goal of finishing this book alongside a range of other goals. I was determined to move ahead and win in every aspect of my life.

By September of that year I was making good progress on most fronts when my mum's health took a turn for the worse and her twin sister was diagnosed with terminal cancer, with only a matter of weeks to live. This also coincided with a big project I was working on, which required me to spend a lot of time away from home. But I was determined not to let these obstacles prevent me fulfilling my goals.

A work colleague who knew me well and was aware of my situation said to me: 'Melanie, is it really feasible to think you can get the book written with everything else going on?' This really made me sit up and think. I started to realise that although it was a noble ambition to attempt to carry on as usual, in reality this was not feasible. Was it my inner critic that was keeping me from being wise about what I could achieve? Was it driving me forward in an attempt to fulfil what were now, given the unexpected circumstances, unrealistic goals? I decided to employ my wisdom and cut myself some slack. After I'd had nearly a year off, my mum was getting the right treatment, life had returned to some sense of normality and I was able to get back to writing.

I am thankful to the colleague who pointed out what was obvious from an outsider's perspective – to a driven person like myself, it seemed at first like 'giving in'. But once I had taken this on board I was able to put the book aside without feeling guilty, knowing that sometime soon it would be the right time to return to it.

Cutting yourself some slack

In the above example I was able to cut myself some slack given all the things that were on my plate at the time. This is something I have often encouraged friends and clients to do: we often forget that we also need to do this from time to time for ourselves. So if you are feeling overwhelmed by your goals, responsibilities – even if they are things you really want to do and enjoy doing – it might be time to cut yourself some slack, to prioritise in order to handle things in a more effective, efficient and enjoyable way.

Q. When could you have cut yourself some slack in the past?

Q. Are there things that it would be wise for you to drop or postpone right now?

What happens if you *don't* cut yourself some slack? From my own experiences and those of my friends the result can be illness, accidents and unhappiness. One friend of mine was rushing around as usual while her mother was dying. She was supporting her parents and working, and it was not until she fell down the stairs and injured her foot that she was given some enforced time to stop and think.

Another friend who had had a hectic week full of juggling work challenges, family life and illnesses was still planning to have a dinner party on the Saturday night. I was challenging her to serve up delicious shop-bought food rather than spending time creating some delight herself, which she usually does. Unfortunately, she never got to rise to the challenge as she fell ill, removing the need to make the decision.

We have a choice: we can either be driven by our inner critic and ignore the messages that our body is sending us and wait for our bodies to force us to stop or ignore the inner critic and make wise decisions. Doing the latter is a far healthier and more satisfying way to learn how to be more realistic and cut ourselves some slack.

We need to learn how to drop things, say no, postpone goals/tasks without guilt. We shouldn't need illnesses and accidents to stop us: instead, we can find a way to do it with grace and confidence. See 'Just say no' later in this Part of the book for more on this.

The result of not cutting ourselves some slack and being unrealistic is that we get stressed and don't enjoy whatever it is we are doing. Or we are not at our best and therefore do not perform as well as we could both at home and at work. What is it that stops you from cutting yourself some slack? Is it thoughts about letting others down, is it about what others will think of you, is it in response to being hounded by your inner critic? What tends to happen to you if you don't cut yourself some slack?

Take an outsider's perspective of your life right now
If you feel overwhelmed by your life and everything you do, it could be because what you are attempting to fit in would overwhelm anyone. Get an outside opinion from someone who you will listen to and respect.

If your wise, supportive friend is not available or it's the middle of the night and you are stressed, anxious or just low, then call on your virtual wise mentors to provide you with an outsider's perspective (see 'Wise words from virtual mentors', Part 2).

What can you drop for now?
There may be things that you set out to do with the best intentions, which for whatever reason are no longer feasible or you're no longer interested in pursuing. Take a deep breath, ignore your inner critic and list the things that you want to drop from your life permanently, and those that you would like to pick up again in the future (near or distant) when the time is right.

Things to drop forever...	Things to drop for now and pick up later...

If you are afraid of dropping things or aren't sure what to drop, then consider the following points:

- What are your key priorities both in and out of work – the 'must dos'
- What activities will in the long run create more time, energy, income and satisfaction?
- What have your inner critic, Fearful Child, Fun Child, Nurturing Parent and Adult got to say about this? Listen to them all. Are some of your fears stopping you from dropping or postponing things?
- What does your wise self think is the most appropriate thing to focus on right now, over the next week or coming months?

Remember that you can always pick things up again in the future and if an opportunity appears to have passed, by creating more realistic goals and 'To Do' lists you will be in a better position to seize future opportunities that arise.

Guilty without a trial

Feeling inferior, guilty or just plain bad – it is amazing that with the help of our inner critic we can do this to ourselves without the assistance of other people. However, as with dealing with criticisms from others, we need to be active in countering the messages from our inner critic.

Our inner critic will often find us guilty without listening to all the evidence; it never gives us the benefit of the doubt and the result is that we often experience full-scale guilt.

We can end up feeling guilty about...

What we have done/not done
What we have said/not said
What we think
What we feel

When we have a strong inner critic, whichever way we turn we are likely to feel guilty about something.

Guilt as wasted emotion

Guilt seems to serve no purpose in this context; even if we have made a mistake, sitting around feeling guilty does not help anyone. Taking action to rectify the mistake and learning from it will be far more positive and empowering.

Most of the time the guilt is not justified, yet it is just as strong as if we had done something. Listening to the different parts of ourselves, as discussed earlier, can be a good way of sorting out what is happening inside our heads and moving on in a positive way.

In Part 2 we explored using real or virtual mentors to assist us and you can consult them to help you deal with mistakes wisely and appropriately. Later in this Part you will come across other techniques which can assist you in dealing with guilt and mistakes. We'll see how using a Brag Bag helps remind you of what you do appreciate about yourself, rather than letting the guilt run away with you, and how Cheerleaders encourage you and counteract the guilty feelings.

Guilt tripping

Some people do seem to revel in their own guilt trips. Being stuck in a guilt trip can be a way of avoiding taking responsibility for the situation in hand and either rectifying what has gone wrong, if anything has, or facing the real issues. However, our fear of facing the facts can inhibit us. Dealing with these fears, rather than ignoring or pandering to them, will help you find a way to move on.

A workshop participant described the process of 'shredding herself', especially if she was awake in the middle of the night worrying or feeling guilty about something. The old inner critic can lead us to almost tear ourselves to pieces, kick ourselves when we are down, just at the moments when we need to have compassion for and support ourselves.

We usually end up kicking ourselves when we are at a low ebb, either physically, emotionally or mentally. It may be that we are tired, ill, hormonal, stressed, made a mistake or suffered a disappointment. It is when our defences are down that the inner critic sees a chink in our armour, goes for it… and it hurts.

'One thing we can admire about ourselves is our resilience. We can be kicked in the face several times, yet still go back for more. We must be careful not to let resilience resemble stupidity.'

Peter Karsten

Learning from mistakes

We are only human and we do make mistakes. Once you have mastered your inner critic you will be able to accept this, learn from the situation, deal with any people involved and get on with the next thing you are facing, rather than being racked by guilt and unable to learn and come to terms with the mistake.

Q. What mistakes have you made in the last six months?
Q. How have you reacted and dealt with them?

'If at first you don't succeed, find out why.'

Stephen R. Covey

When we realise we have made a mistake either through feedback from others or our own realisations, two things can stop us from accepting and learning from what has happened:

We feel threatened

The inner critic coupled with feedback from others can feel quite threatening. In fact even if only our inner critic is involved we can still experience the 'flight or fight' reaction and feel threatened.

What to do to counter this

Take a deep breath, mentally step back and reflect on the situation. If someone else is giving you the feedback, ask for a short break to enable you to calm down the natural adrenaline rush and start to listen to and explore the feedback you are receiving.

We feel foolish

All too often we recognise the truth of what is being said, or what we have realised for ourselves, but waste our energies and our thoughts on feeling foolish, embarrassed and/or guilty.

What to do to counter this

We can find out exactly what happened and what we could do about it. Being able to realistically and constructively debrief yourself (see 'Debriefing using your wisdom', Part 2) will enable you to go beyond feeling foolish and learn from the experience and/or feedback.

Once you have learned how to master your inner critic, and you are connecting more with your Adult self, you will find it easier to learn from mistakes without the guilt trip. There was an instance recently in a voluntary organisation that I work for. A decision was made that some people were unhappy about. Talking to one person I realised that we had overlooked something, and although we could not go back to change what had happened, I was able to genuinely apologise for the mistake and make sure that we learned from it.

'There are no mistakes, no coincidences. All events are blessings given to us to learn from.'

Elisabeth Kübler-Ross

Forgiving yourself

When was the last time you forgave yourself for something you did or said? We are only human... sometimes during coaching sessions I have clients giving themselves a hard time because they slip back into old patterns of behaviour or don't do as well as they had hoped in a situation. The tyranny of perfectionism (see Part 3) comes in here, along with the delusion that one day we will have got it all sorted and be that perfect human being who never gets it wrong.

But as human beings we have good and bad days, bad nights' sleep, illnesses, stresses in our home and work life, which put pressure on us. Our ability to be our best can be sorely stretched.

Being the best you can be given the circumstances

Nowadays I find it more helpful to think about how I can be the best I can given the circumstances I find myself in. So I don't give in and say, 'Well, I had a bad night and so it is going to be a difficult day.' Instead I say, 'I had a bad night, so what do I need to do today to support myself so I can be the best I can, given this?' Basically, I cut myself some slack, but at the same time I look at things I can do (many of which are in this book) to resource and support myself to keep on going and do as good a job as possible given the circumstances.

Taking an adult approach to mistakes

'Mistakes are a fact of life. It is the response to error that counts.'
Nikki Giovanni

When we are growing up most of us do not learn how to take an Adult approach to mistakes. When we are young and we make mistakes it usually elicits a negative Critical Parent response from the elders around us. We respond to this by feeling guilty, bad, fearful. The end result is that as adults we tend to either hide mistakes and not take responsibility for them, or feel bad about them and fail to learn from them.

Over the last few years I have learned how empowering it is to respond to mistakes and issues from my Adult mode. I will often be the first to admit when I have done something wrong, when there appears to be a communication breakdown with clients, a mistake in a document or some other error. It is strange that sometimes this honesty leads to a debate, with the other person saying 'No, I am sure it was my mistake.' People are not used to someone taking ownership of mistakes.

Just say no!

'Only robots can say no without feeling guilty.'
Anne Dickson

'Just say no!' Not so easy, is it? We say yes to requests for help, work we would rather not do, dinner parties we would rather not go to. This can result in us feeling overloaded and overwhelmed by what is on our plate, or burdened by the expectations of colleagues, friends and family.

What stops you saying no without guilt? Ask yourself the following questions and think about how many apply to you:

- Are there certain times, situations and places where you feel it is easier to say no and others where it seems much harder or even impossible? Perhaps you can do it at work, but not at home, or vice versa; you can say no to friends but not your parents or your boss; you can say no when you are happy and on top of things but not when you feel stretched and exhausted?

- Do you simply not know how to say no in a straightforward way? Perhaps you go into overlong explanations when you say no? Or do you end up volunteering even when you haven't been asked?

- When you think about saying no, do you get negative pictures in your head of people getting angry or being hurt? Do you have messages going through your head about letting people down, not being liked, being pathetic or lazy? These pictures and messages can have a profound effect on how you feel and on your behaviour.

- Do you believe that in some situations it is impossible to say no? Perhaps you believe that others will not respect you or like you if you say no. If you do have negative beliefs like this about saying no they are likely to stop you from doing so.

- Are you so dragged down by your busyness and saying yes the whole time that it is hard to muster the energy to say no? Does it just seem easier to say yes? Perhaps you see yourself as being 'the busy one' or 'the helpful one' and wonder who you will be if you start to say no to things.

The challenge of saying no

My experience is that just when I think I have learned to say no, another situation comes up to challenge me. As my natural reaction is to be helpful and say yes, I have to constantly be on my guard so that I think before I respond. For example, if I receive an e-mail about an event that I could get involved in on a voluntary basis, rather than giving my response immediately, I simply reply and say I will get back to them and let them know. This gives me time to engage my wise self and decide whether it's appropriate to say yes or no.

Some of us are so conditioned to please others that we need to consider how to balance that with pleasing rather than overloading ourselves.

Q. What do you want to say no to? Or what do you want to stop doing?

Q. What will be the benefits to you of doing this? What will it feel like? What will your life be like?

Q. How might others react?

Q. How will you deal with their reaction so that it does not get in the way of you saying no?

Stop and think – is this wise?

Stop before you say yes or volunteer for something. Stop and ask yourself what is driving your behaviour. What mode is this coming from – your inner critic, Adult, Fearful Child or wise self? How will taking on this task or responsibility benefit you? What will be the negative effects of taking it on?

If your 'Yes' or decision to volunteer your time is going to enhance your life, and is coming from your wise self, then go ahead. If you are doing it out of guilt, or because of any 'shoulds' or because you are finding it hard to say no, stop, take time out to listen to your wise self and make sure you are making the wisest decision possible.

Play for time

Our inner critic with all its overbearing nature often expects us to say yes here and now. But the wisest thing to do is to ask for time to think it over before answering. Say you need to consult your diary, check with your partner, check on your other commitments. This will give you time to stop and think about the wisest thing to do.

Being prepared for others' reactions

If people are used to you saying yes the whole time they might have a negative reaction to you saying no, especially if they have come to rely on you to always step in and help out. They might just be surprised and taken aback by your new stance, or they might take it personally. Depending on your relationship with them you might want to elaborate on why you are saying no in this instance.

Elicit the support of your mentors

If you feel guilty it can be useful to elicit the views of your mentors, real or virtual, to assist you in thinking through what you want to take on and what you want to say no to.

Visualise yourself saying no

If the idea of saying no seems like an impossibility, either in general or in a specific situation, visualising yourself doing it can be very powerful and assist you in taking the necessary action in real life. Visualise how your life will be if you say yes or no. See what you look like, what your life looks like, hear how you sound, feel what it will be like. Imagine how good you will feel saying no to someone without guilt. (The process of visualisation is described in more detail in Part 4.)

Fun, frolics and celebrations

Our inner critic takes life very seriously and tends to want to put a stop to any frivolity or celebrations, with the result that some people never appreciate their successes and how far they have developed, or they rarely relax enough to smile and laugh. This section encourages you to celebrate who you are and what you do, and generally encourages you to have more fun.

Brag bags and glad rags

Once I was running a self-management programme for field salespeople and we were talking about how we motivate ourselves. One of the participants said that he had a Brag File where he put all his certificates and letters of thanks from clients and his manager. Those of us with inner critics at first recoiled at the idea of this 'boasting', but afterwards I decided to adapt his idea and created by own 'Brag Bag', though don't ask me why it is called a Brag Bag as it has always been a small colourful notebook.

What is in a Brag Bag?

A Brag Bag is somewhere you can list what you appreciate about yourself. When I first started keeping a Brag Bag I did it almost daily, then at least weekly, and I have managed to get through several small notebooks. The idea is that the process will help you to appreciate yourself: eventually you should be able to do so without having to go through the process of writing it down. Nowadays I only write in there if my inner critic has reared its ugly head again; in fact, the last time I used it was a couple of years ago.

Here is a sample of some of the things you could add to your Brag Bag:

I appreciate myself for:
- Exercising three times this week.
- Eating sensibly most of the time!
- Handling some difficult questions during a meeting.
- Taking time out to enjoy the sunset.
- Supporting my family.
- Getting the report done on time when the deadline was so tight.

It does not matter what form or structure your Brag Bag takes as long as it is positive and affirms who you are and what you do.

It is a good idea to keep your Brag Bags so that at times when your inner critic is having a go at you, you can look back and see all the great things you have appreciated about yourself in the past. Also, looking back often serves as a record of how much you have changed and what you have achieved, thereby countering any 'glass-is-half-full' thinking if you feel you are not making any progress.

Common mortals need praise

I have the following quote from Nichiren Daishonin, a thirteenth-century Buddhist, at the beginning of my Brag Bags notebooks:

> *'When one is praised highly by others, one feels there is no hardship he cannot bear. Such is the courage which springs from words of praise... when criticised, one can recklessly cause one's own ruin. Such is the way of common mortals.'*

Although this quote is about people praising each other, it equally applies to us praising ourselves. We are all common mortals and we respond well to praise. Criticism only creates unhappiness and lack of self worth, and hinders our progress. So let's praise and appreciate ourselves for what we do, rather than focussing on what we don't do.

Think about the last month: what do you appreciate about yourself? Write down at least ten 'appreciations'.

'Yes but...'

You may find your inner critic saying 'Yes but what about X that you haven't done?' or 'What about when you said Y in that meeting when you should have kept your mouth shut?' When this happens remember that you can praise yourself while still working on the things you want to change. And you can celebrate your progress even if you have not achieved the goals you have set out for yourself. Praising yourself will lead you to feeling good about yourself, you will feel more motivated and capable of doing whatever else you need to do.

Pride before a fall

There might be a part of you that is feeling uncomfortable with all this stuff about praise – you might even have the expression 'Pride comes before a fall' running through your head. If so, you might want to take a look at Part 4 on Mastering Your Mind for the exercise on transforming your beliefs, as you might be holding onto beliefs that are getting in the way of you feeling proud about yourself or accepting praise from yourself and others. You can be proud of yourself, your life and your achievements, while still being modest.

Practice makes perfect

The more you practise this process of appreciating yourself, the easier it will become. It can become part of how you approach life. In fact, my Brag Bag has almost become redundant as I can appreciate myself without having to refer to it. However, at first it can be difficult. I remember introducing the idea many years ago to a group of young women when we were attending a course together. A lot of them were beating themselves up so I introduced the idea of 'appreciations'. Many of them found it very difficult to do at first, as they were so unused to the idea. It is definitely a case of 'practice makes perfect'.

Bring on the cheerleaders

During a session with my personal coach, I was talking about my inner critic and he suddenly asked me who my favourite actor was. I said George Clooney (well, there were reruns of ER on TV at the time...) and he suggested that whenever my inner critic spoke up, I should imagine George whispering the criticisms into my ear.

Well, of course, whenever I imagine that it just makes me laugh, and dear old George would never say anything horrible to me. Also, when I imagine this I get a sensation and a picture of him standing to my left whispering into my ear – as you can guess, a fairly pleasant sensation! So it takes the heat out of those inner critic messages.

I've now taken this idea further and George is joined by some other significant people in my life (friends and colleagues who are always supportive) who would only say nice things to me. They fight for space on my left-hand side, shouting positive things if I ever start to be nasty to myself. I call these voices my 'cheerleaders'.

Cheerleaders are vibrant

If you think about cheerleaders in their natural setting, cheering on their team, they are loud, colourful and vibrant. My cheerleaders might not be dressed up in the outfits, but they do jump around a lot, waving their arms and cheering me on. So make sure yours are as animated as possible. I find that the moment I bring them on they make me smile or laugh as they are so lively and enthusiastic. They say things like:

'Oh no, you're not... [whatever the inner critic has been saying to me], you're wonderful, caring, clever...' [whatever I need to hear at the time]
'You're great, remember the time you did such and such.'
'We love Melanie, rah, rah, rah!!!'

Who are your cheerleaders?

They can be people you know, historical people you admire or even fictional characters – anyone you can rely on to always say positive things.

Remember: cheerleaders are there to cheer you on through the highs and lows, not just to celebrate your successes. So make sure that you bring them on whenever you need cheering up or you need to counter your inner critic.

Here are some examples of when you might use your cheerleaders:

- You catch yourself beating yourself up about a mistake you have made.
- You're preparing to go on a date and aren't feeling your most confident.
- You feel stuck and can't find a way round a particular problem.
- Someone praises you and you feel a fraud.

Q. When can you use them to help support yourself?

Q. What past situations could you have used them in?

Q. In what future situations could you bring on your cheerleaders?

If I've got to start somewhere, I'll start with the encouragement. Bring on the Cheerleaders!

TO DO LIST

Celebrating success and change

Life can be quite demoralising if we don't acknowledge the changes that have happened, how far we've come and what has gone well. Instead, the inner critic can make you focus on how far you still have to go or your weaker points, leading to frustration and demotivation.

If you celebrate your progress and the changes that do occur you will feel more energised, enthusiastic and motivated to keep on until you have either changed what you wanted to change or reached your goal.

So go ahead and ignore your inner critic, celebrate what you do get done and the steps along the way…

Speeding up the celebration process

Break activities/projects into small steps – this makes them more achievable, as you will be motivated to achieve each bit, and satisfied when you do. The steps might vary depending on what you are undertaking:

- Doing a work task you have put off for ages – it is often those important but non-urgent tasks that will make your life easier but are a bit dull to do that get put off forever. Identify the first two or three steps and break down to manageable chunks of 20 minutes to an hour.
- Getting fit and healthy – finding out the times of the gym/swimming session; attending the gym/swim three times a week; being able to fit into a particular outfit easily and comfortable; losing a certain amount of weight a month; being able to run for the bus without getting breathless.
- Learning a language – break it down into simple yet significant words and phrases you want to learn; think about specific situations where you want to be able to communicate and learn words associated with them.
- Writing a report or dissertation – getting the contents mapped out, jotting down ideas for different sections, writing sections, editing it, checking spellings and facts, writing the bibliography.

With any undertaking, if you only have the end product or goal in your sights success can seem a very long way off and it can seem like a very long slog to get there.

What projects, tasks, activities, and endeavours are you undertaking that you could benefit from breaking into smaller steps? Remember to have mini celebrations or at least praise yourself along the way!

Write down the end goal first: lose a stone in weight, write a report, run a marathon, apply for a new job.

Break the activity into manageable parts that can be done in a short space of time. This could be 10 or 20 minute chunks depending on your own attention span and motivation.

Now think of a reward for each part that you achieve and a special reward at the end.

Celebrate your progress

Take time to celebrate what has gone well and the changes you have made as you progress towards your goal. If you meet obstacles or you make mistakes along the way (which is inevitable in life), then determine to learn from the experiences. Relax and celebrate where you have succeeded and what you have learned so far. If you are a 'glass-is-half-empty' person it is easy to fall into the trap of feeling you can't relax and enjoy your progress if something does not go 100 per cent to plan.

Rewarding yourself

Setting rewards that you work towards when you have achieved different stages on the way towards your goal can act as a motivator. If the goal itself is not that exciting but will bring long-term benefits, some rewards along the way can keep you going.

I was having a conversation with a colleague of mine about different ways of rewarding ourselves. She said that she had got into the habit of rewarding herself with a nice meal out after completing a challenging piece of work. She then realised that what she really valued from the meal out on her own was time to herself without the pressures of work and her two young sons. She decided that a coffee and a read of the paper would be just as rewarding and not as expensive.

Q. Do you reward yourself for the successes you have or the progress that you are making?

Q. What can you use as rewards?

Releasing your Fun Child

When was the last time you laughed until you cried or your sides ached? When was the last time you were silly or you danced until your legs hurt? When was the last time your Fun Child had a good time?

For some people this will happen quite often. For others, the times of having unadulterated fun are limited or completely squashed out by the pressures of work, family commitments and daily chores – or by our inner critic.

What stops the Fun Child having fun?

Frequently it is the inner critic that gets in the way of this, with comments like:

'That is childish.'
'You're an adult now and you should behave like one.'
'There are more important things to get on with.'
'But we still haven't done X, Y and Z.'
'Tomorrow, next month, next year we can do that.'

While the Fun Child, if you listen to him or her, is probably saying:

'Oh please can we have an ice cream, swing on the swings, go dancing and be silly for once!'
'Please let's have time to just chill and not be serious for once.'
'I want to have some fun now!'

The inner critic can have such a strong hold that the Fun Child never gets a look in. Even when times are hard you need to make sure there is some unadulterated fun to be had, in fact this is especially important when times are hard, as you will be re-energised by laughter and fun.

If not now, when? Releasing the energy now

I was running a session for a women's network and a woman said in response to a discussion about the Fun Child: 'But there is always more to be done, there is no time to stop and have fun.' My reaction is: 'If not now, when?' There will always be things to do, and if you wait for the eternal To Do list to be ticked off you will wait a long time. Once you have experienced the surge in energy and motivation by 'giving in to', 'pandering' or just allowing some Fun Child time you will recognise the huge benefits this brings. If you never give it a go, you will never recognise and experience these benefits.

Who killed the Fun Child?

What has become apparent from running my workshops on 'Mastering Your Inner Critic' is that for some people the Fun Child has never been allowed to develop. Some participants have talked about different reasons for this connected with their childhoods:

- They spent their childhood in poverty and life was far too hard for them to be allowed to be frivolous.

- There was illness in their family, so they had to 'grow up' quickly, and laughter and lightness was missing from their childhood.
- Their parents were, as a result of their own upbringing, plagued with their own fears and found it hard to allow their children to run free and have fun.
- At school, a particular teacher's critical nature fed into their inner critic, leaving little to smile about.

Not everyone with an inner critic has lost or failed to develop their Fun Child as we have all had different experiences that have got us to where we are today.

Learning to smile again

What I have noticed in those people whose Fun Child had either not developed or been lost along the way is the lack of smiles. It is hard to smile if your inner critic is continually having a go at you and/or your Fearful Child is constantly wary of what might happen next. When the inner critic is under control and the Fearful Child is being cared for it will be easier for the Fun Child to naturally appear and for the smiles to return.

Fun times come in different packages

'Be a kid once in a while and have some unadulterated fun.'
Peter Karsten

A couple of times a year I go with friends to our local comedy club. This is a great combination of entertainment, laughter, dancing and letting our hair down. On two occasions when friends have had to leave to relieve babysitters I have stayed on dancing on my own, like a child not ready to leave the party and go back to normal life. One particular time I was there got me thinking about our Fun Child and how often we get to indulge it.

Think about times when your Fun Child has come out to play – perhaps it was unexpectedly or in some unusual circumstances.

I remember being out walking with my mum quite a few years ago and coming across a playground which no one was using. After we had been on the swings for a bit, I decided to go down the slide, not noticing the very end was missing and not realising that being heavier than a child I might end up going further than a child. My mum said the expression on my face was so funny as I shot off the end and we ended up killing ourselves laughing about it.

I also have a photo of my dad's smiling face above a huge milkshake that I took when I took him for a birthday treat in London. He had not had a milkshake since childhood, and the ones he had had were certainly not like this one!

Fun with friends

It is so important to have friends to laugh with, both in the good and bad times. With my great friend Ali, we always end up laughing at the end of a conversation, even if at the beginning one of us is in a hell of a state and crying. Fun friends are those that you can laugh with, be silly at times, who have a sense of humour that lightens life. Make sure that you spend time with your fun friends on a regular basis or at least speak to them on the phone for some light relief. Think of different things you can do with your friends to create more fun times. Every person will have their own fun activities that they like to do with friends, but here are a few ideas to inspire you:

- Have a games evening – revisit some of the games of your childhood as well as new ones.
- Murder mystery parties can be great fun if everyone dresses up and gets into character – one way to leave your cares behind for an evening.
- Birthday parties and surprises – so many adults get into the mind set of 'I'm too old to celebrate birthdays, what

is there to celebrate anyway?' Well, how about a great excuse for a party and some fun?

- Fireworks – as children, most of us once we overcame our fear of fireworks were in awe of them. Recreate some of that childlike wonder with fireworks on birthdays, New Year and other occasions.
- Movie nights – at home or at the cinema, gather together with popcorn and a good comedy.

Fun times

When can you have some fun? Is it saved up for special occasions?

Weekday fun

Think about how you can create fun times during the week that will generate laughter and re-energise you. It might be a mid-week movie (at home or out), a special meal, even half an hour of playtime with the kids after homework and before bed. I've just taken up ceroc dancing and there is lots of laughter as us newbies get in a tangle while attempting to jive.

Weekends full of fun

If your weekends are full of chores or ferrying the children around, then think how you can change this. How can you create fun at the weekends even if there are chores to be done? Are you putting off seeing friends or doing fun things to catch up on work? What can you do during the week to create more space at the weekends? Part of the Fun Child can be about just chilling out, having no responsibilities for once, no timetables to work to. So, create some space for yourself, and your family if you have one, to just chill, with nowhere to go, nothing urgent to do. Are you too tired come the weekend to do anything? Think about what you can do to energise and nurture yourself so that you have the energy for fun times. If you have children, think about how you can take time out to have fun with them. One mother explained to me that she had four weekends in a row when her son was at birthday parties. Great for him, but not so much fun for her, as she spent most of the time in the car.

Holidays
Fortunately for children nowadays there are so many different things that they can do during their holidays whether they are at home or away somewhere. Gone are the days when six weeks loomed ahead with a sindy doll, a bike and some friends to occupy you. But what about the parents or people without children? Are you too exhausted from work to unwind and enjoy your holidays? Or do you even skip them, because you have too much work to do or think they are more hassle than they are worth. Be creative and think about how can you plan a holiday that is fun, within your budget and leaves you feeling refreshed, motivated and ready to throw yourself back into the rest of your life.

What would be fun things for you to do that would delight your inner Fun Child?
What did you do in the past that you used to enjoy and could do again?
Write a list of the fun things that you can do in the next 12 months.

Don't let your logical self spoil your fun
When we are busy and pressured it is easy for either our logical or critical mind to talk us out of some activities. One autumn I had promised my Fun Child a day by the sea and had pencilled

in a particular Saturday. When the day arrived my logical self said: 'But it is so far to go, it will cost too much in petrol, it's not environmentally friendly, the days are too short, it's not worth going.' And I nearly listened to her. But the weather forecast was good and my Fun Child was up for it and I decided to go. The moment I decided I was filled with unexpected excitement; I was going somewhere I had never been before and did not know what to expect. What I found was an amazing walk along a spit with the sea on one side, saltwater marshes on the other and, much to my surprise, a castle at the end! The sky was blue, the surf was up and it was gorgeous. At the end of the day I sat in a cafe watching the sun set over the sea feeling very content and happy.

The added bonus is that whenever I tell anyone about it I again experience the joy, excitement and energy that came from that day away.

> 'It is not the world that makes you unhappy, or the way people are in the world. It's how you process the people and events of the world.'
>
> Dr Wayne W. Dyer

Part 4

Managing Your Mood

'You will have no inner peace as long as the controls of your life are located outside yourself.'

Dr Wayne W. Dyer

Why is managing your mood important for mastering your inner critic? Because the inner critic has a tendency to kick us when we are down, when we are in a low life state or negative mood. Being able to manage your mood and keep your spirits up will assist you in the process of mastering your inner critic.

This Part contains two sections:

Changing your mood
The first step is to learn to recognise the moods that you experience and the fact that you can do something to change them. Then you will learn techniques to transform your mood and be more positive about yourself and your life.

Mastering your mind
What you think and the beliefs you hold have a profound effect on how you feel and your behaviour. Learning techniques to assist

you in mastering your mind will enable you to take control of your moods and therefore your inner critic.

Changing Your Mood

This section will enable you to gain a greater understanding of your own moods and what you can do to manage them as you go through your day. You will learn simple techniques to enable you to feel more positive, tap into your inner resources and transform negative moods when they occur.

Understanding your mood

You may have noticed that often when we ask someone how they are, they say things like fine, OK, tired, stressed – but this does not necessarily tell you the whole story. We often tell people about the emotion or mood that is on top, but we are much more complex than that. There is much more to one's mood than a single emotion. There are not only positive and negative moods, but also low and high energy ones, and they all have a different impact on how we think, how we react to situations and how we behave.

The inner critic and mood

Often it is when we are in a negative mood that our inner critic goes in for the attack, although for some people the inner critic can also kick in when they are feeling positive and happy with comments such as 'What have you got to be happy about?', 'It won't last, you'll end up crying,' and so forth. Either way, being able to understand, identify and name your emotions is the starting point to learning how to manage them and your inner critic.

The following Mood Map will assist you in understanding the range of moods you might be experiencing at any one time.

How are you right now?

On the Mood Map below tick the words that best describe how you feel right now. Tick as many as you like. Some may even seem to contradict each other, as we have lots of different things going on in our lives, which can create different moods within us. You can feel calm in the present moment, while still being anxious about something else that is going on in your life. Feel free to add moods that might better describe how you feel.

High Energy

Lively	Angry
Healthy	Rebellious
Excited	Flustered
Enthusiastic	Ashamed
Energetic	Uncertain
Interested	Tense
Determined	Anxious
Friendly	Panicky
Sociable	Nervous
Alert	Afraid
Talkative	Frustrated

Positive ━━━━━━━━━━━━━━━━━━━━ **Negative**

Calm	Worn out
Relaxed	Bored
Satisfied	Tired
Centred	Fed up
Trusting	Lonely
Content	Sorry
Happy	Gloomy
Pleased	Down
Satisfied	Helpless

Low Energy

What do you do with these moods?

'Instead of allowing ourselves to be led and trapped by our feelings, we should let them disappear as soon as they form, like letters drawn on water with a finger.'

Dilgo Khyentse Rinpoche

I love this idea of letting go of moods as soon as they form. But, like most people, I have not yet achieved this state of mastery over my feelings, to be able to just let go of them as easy as they come. Sometimes it is possible, but at other times I need to do more to deal with the feelings and moods I am experiencing.

If we use the mood map, most of us will find that we experience a range of emotions at any one time. But how do the different types of emotions impact on you and what can you do to transform them if they are having a negative impact? It seems to be a fact of life that the inner critic will kick you when you are at your lowest, so managing your mood is another way of combating the inner critic.

It is the nature of life that moods will go up and down. However, we can become more aware of our moods, the impact they have on our lives and how to manage them, especially when we are facing difficult circumstances.

Negative low-energy mood

Did you end up ticking a lot of these compared to the other sectors? Their impact can be draining and demoralising, especially over long periods, so it is important to look at how you support yourself. Activities that will help you to rest, relax, and recuperate, that generally provide you with some TLC, will help you to deal with and move out of these low-energy negative states. The part on Supporting Yourself will help you to explore what activities you can do to nurture and revive yourself.

It is important to pace yourself if you are in a low-energy negative mood, rather than let your inner critic bully you about the state you are in, which is likely to result in you feeling even lower and more demoralised. For more about this see 'Pacing Yourself', Part 5.

Negative high-energy mood

Have you noticed how if you feel angry, frustrated or anxious it is very difficult to concentrate on other things? These high-energy moods take up a lot of mental and physical energy. There are two aspects of dealing with them:

Deal with the underlying cause as soon as possible

If you are angry, find a way to calm down enough to be able to take appropriate and constructive action. If you are anxious then get to the bottom of your anxiety by either listening to the different parts of you (see Part 3) or talking to a friend, coach or counsellor to help you deal with your anxieties. The longer you leave these negative high-energy emotions the more they will consume your energy and your mind. I have a friend who often gets stuck in emotional states about things that have happened at work or within her family. Instead of spending some time working through the emotions in herself, and then with the individuals concerned, she will spend weeks if not months feeling angry and aggrieved about something. This definitely impinges on other aspects of her life. So rather than hold onto the negative emotions and let them ruin your day, week or year, find ways of dealing with the issue in hand and then you will be able to move on.

Release the energy in a positive way

Sometimes the root of the problem is not easy to solve. Some things can't be 'fixed': we have to learn to live with them. But at times they can cause all kinds of emotions. You can get to the point where you just want to scream. Having dealt with many ongoing health concerns within my family that I have no control over, I do get to the stage when I feel like screaming. To avoid ending up screaming at someone else, I find screaming my head off in the car (not at anyone, so there is no road rage involved) is very therapeutic! It is the one place you can scream as loud as you want and no one can hear you. Try it. The release of energy is amazing. Sometimes after a long scream I still find that there is some pent up energy, so I have another scream and that usually does the trick. It does not solve the underlying cause, but it goes a long way to releasing the pent up negative energy. A number of workshop participants have now tried this technique and find it very therapeutic.

> *'Screaming under strict guidelines can be quite beneficial to one's sanity.'*
> Peter Karsten

A friend of mine started work with a personal trainer, and she found the best bit of it was doing kick boxing – she said it was the best way of getting rid of the frustrations she was feeling without harming anyone!

Other people find a good workout in the gym, a game of squash, singing in a band or shouting at your team on the terraces releases the negative energies that have built up over the day or week equally well. If those don't appeal to you then hit a cushion or even better have a pillow fight with someone – you will probably end up laughing. The most important thing is to release the energy in a positive way that does not harm you or anyone else.

Write a list of things that you can do to release negative energy. When you start to experience these emotions take action to release the negative energy.

Positive low-energy mood

These are very pleasant and enjoyable states to be in – they are positive, but being low energy they allow us to relax and recuperate from the stresses of life. Think back to times when you have had moments of contentment, calmness or happiness, even if they were just a moment in time. Although we enjoy the buzz of high-energy positive moods, we need low-energy positive ones as well. It is worth looking at the Mood Map and thinking about whether you allow yourself the time and place to luxuriate in these moods. Our inner critic can sometimes be responsible for keeping us so busy, urging us onto the next task or goal, that we never have time to stop and feel a sense of satisfaction, contentment or calm. Sometimes it can be about just taking five minutes out as you go through your day to have moments of calm.

Q. When was the last time you experienced these kinds of low-energy positive moods?

Q. What can you do to create more space to experience these emotions?

Upping the tempo

Although it is good to experience these low-energy positive moods, sometimes we need to up the tempo to have the energy to do certain things in life. If I am getting ready to go out in the evening, I will often put on some upbeat party music to get me in the mood. If I am about to run a workshop with a lively group of participants who like a good laugh I know I need to up my energy levels to match theirs.

Positive high-energy mood

These moods are energising, and can even give you enough energy to deal with the most difficult aspects of life. The reality of life is that we will not stay in high-energy positive moods forever. In fact for most of us that would be quite tiring. What we need to aim for is a mixture of high- and low-energy positive moods to help offset the negative ones we will inevitably face.

Do you want to change how you feel right now?

There is a simple exercise that demonstrates that what you focus on influences how you feel. You can transform how you feel right now. This exercise will only take a few minutes to complete.

Step 1

Think of something you really don't like or even hate doing (either at home or at work). Close your eyes, as this will help you to do the exercise, and see yourself in that situation, hear whatever there is to hear, feel what it feels like – stay with this just long enough to notice any changes in how you are feeling, then bring yourself back to the present moment.

Step 2

Now think about how you feel having thought about this thing that you don't like. Most people report that they experienced feelings of anger, frustration, demotivation, sadness, anxiety or some other equally strong negative emotion. Now rather than stay with those negative emotions let's move onto Step 3…

Step 3

Think of something that you really enjoy doing, or a place you love to be. Again close your eyes if that helps. See yourself in that situation or doing the thing that you like to do, hear everything there is to hear, and feel how it makes you feel. You can stay doing this as long as you wish.

Step 4

Now think about how you feel having thought about this thing that you really like. Notice how differently the two situations make you feel. During Step 3 most people are quickly able to access feelings of joy, calmness, satisfaction, enthusiasm, excitement or other strong positive emotions.

So without going anywhere people are able to change their state, by changing what they focus on. They can go from neutral to intensely negative emotions to very strong positive ones in a matter of minutes. That is the power we can have over our minds and we can harness this to master our inner critics.

Daily mood management

How does your mood affect your day? Is your behaviour and performance affected by your moods? What part does your inner critic play in affecting your mood on a day-by-day basis?

A friend once told me that he had spent a whole weekend in a state of anxiety over a big meeting he had to chair on the following Monday. This was mainly because his inner critic was not allowing him to see his strengths and the years of experience he was bringing to what was going to be a fairly difficult meeting.

Shortly afterwards I met up with a colleague on her way back home from a very successful workshop, where she had decided to trust her instincts (and considerable experience and skills) and conduct the workshop in a very innovative way. The event had gone particularly well and as she drove home she was congratulating herself on how well she had conducted the event. But then she started to doubt herself. She wondered whether she should be analysing whether things could have been done even better or differently.

Both of these instances got me thinking that there are actions that we can take before, during and after activities that can help us to prepare, take part in and debrief in a constructive and supportive manner, rather than let our inner critics drive our preparation and the review of activities in a destructive way.

It's been a bit easier since

I found the controls to
my emotional thermostat!

Managing your own mood

Think about your daily life, either during your working week or at the weekends. There may be actions that you take consciously or unconsciously that help you to manage your mood and therefore control your inner critic.

You will find that the greater the range of supports you use the better able you will be to manage your mood and your inner critic.

Think about the actions that you take at the beginning, during and at the end of each day to support yourself and manage your mood. Write these down. Are there additional things that you could do?

When I do this exercise during workshops people have a range of activities or simple things that they do to help support themselves through their working day or during challenging times. For example:

Before	During	After
Walking the dog.	Taking time out over lunch.	Walking the dog.
Listening to certain music while travelling to work – to calm them down or energise them.	Going for a short walk.	Going to the gym.
	Reading a book during a break.	Having a relaxing bath.
Eating a good breakfast.	Chatting with colleagues about non-work things.	Having a drink.
Taking a few minutes to themselves before starting the day.	Having a laugh.	Going out with friends.
		Talking to a good friend.
Meditating, carrying out some kind of spiritual practice.	Visualising success if they start to feel negative.	Playing with their children.
		Having ten-minute slots each with their partner to sound off about their day.

Being in the best possible mood

There are other things that you can do before, during and after events to manage your mood. In fact, there are a number of techniques in this book that I use on a regular basis to ensure that I am in the best possible mood, regardless of what is going on in my life.

From my experience of learning to manage my moods I feel that we owe it to ourselves, our families, friends, colleagues – in fact, whoever we are going to be interacting with that day – to be in the best possible state. The old me, who went through life in a fairly low life state most of the time, did not realise that I could do something about it. In the past if things were going badly and I was in a bad mood, then it was given that I would have a bad day. Do you resign yourself to a 'bad day' or are you able to turn it around?

Nowadays I am not willing to accept that kind of life. If I wake up and am less than positive then I will do something to transform this. If I falter through the day, I will again do something to help me. And if at the end of the day my spirits start to flag for some reason I will once more take action to make sure that I end the day on as good a note as possible. Take a look at the ideas over the next few pages and see if you want to add anything to your list of activities you can do before, during and at the end of your day to manage your mood.

Actions to take beforehand, at the beginning of the day

Check in with yourself first thing in the morning

This might sound an obvious thing to do, but a lot of people lead such busy lives and are so busy 'doing' that they lose touch with how they are and what they are feeling. Find a time that suits you: it might be when you wake up before you get out of bed; it could be in the shower; it might be just as you are about to leave the house for work or while travelling to work. Stop and think about what mood you are in.

Create a positive outcome

Before I undertake a particular event or activity I find it useful to write down in positive terms what I want to achieve. This focuses the mind on a positive outcome (rather than your fears) and means you will be clearer about what you want to achieve in a particular situation.

Visualise success

Once you have created your positive outcome it can be helpful to simply look up and visualise whatever it is that you are wanting to do. By visualising yourself being successful in a situation you are going to feel more upbeat and motivated than if you end up thinking about all the things that could go wrong.

Transform your beliefs

Beliefs can have a powerful impact on how we feel and behave, so it is worthwhile becoming aware of them, spotting those that are hindering you in a situation and taking action to create new, more helpful beliefs (see the exercise 'Transforming your beliefs' at the end of this Part of the book to assist you). You might wake up thinking: 'Whatever I do at work today it won't make a difference', or 'I'm hopeless, I'm never going to be able to do X or Y.' Instead of letting these beliefs slip you up you can transform them into more positive beliefs, creating a better mood and a better day.

Resource yourself

If you are feeling less than resourceful and confident you might like to remind yourself of all the great inner resources that you have within you that the inner critic might lead you to ignore: your courage, determination, sense of humour and so on (see 'Inner resources' later in this Part). By accessing these 'hidden' resources you face the day in a more positive mood.

Physical readiness
Consider what you do for yourself physically before work or challenging times. Are you eating healthily? Are you drinking sensibly? Are you starting the day with a breakfast that sets you up for your day ahead? Are you doing everything possible to get a good night's sleep? What can you do to make sure you are in the best possible state physically?

Emotional readiness
The techniques described above will assist you with being emotionally ready for your day ahead, but in addition you might find it useful to listen to the different parts of yourself first thing in the morning (see Part 3). This will mean that rather than just waking up to the inner critic, you listen to any hopes and fears that other parts of you might have.

Spiritual readiness
This can be about whatever raises your spirits, rather than an actual spiritual practice. People often talk about listening to certain music to get them in the right mood for the day ahead; some find walking the dog a good way to immerse themselves in nature first thing in the morning, while others might prefer to read an inspirational quotation or book.

Actions to take during your day, an event or a situation

Check in with yourself as you go through the day
Notice how you feel, spot when you go off-centre. The quicker you can do this, the easier it will be to take action to bring yourself back into a positive state. This comes with practice. Watch out for physical changes in your body: a tensing of your shoulders

or your neck, a headache, a sinking feeling in your stomach or some other physical change that indicates you are no longer in a confident, positive mood. What physical signs do you notice in yourself when you are slipping into a less than positive state?

Look up

This is a quick way of getting out of a negative mood or state. Where we look results in us accessing different parts of our brain. By looking up you are accessing your visual cortex, which has two benefits. Firstly, it is almost impossible to experience a negative emotion while looking up and therefore it forces you to feel more positive. Secondly, when you look up and access your visual cortex it is much easier to visualise how you are going to handle things. This is very useful if you are starting to feel anxious, stressed, angry or under-confident in a particular situation. For more about the visualisation process see 'Visualising success', later in this Part of the book.

Disassociate yourself

Being fully associated with good emotions and in the moment when we are enjoying ourselves is a good thing. However, if we start to experience negative emotions and we stay fully associated with them, we can become overwhelmed by them. If you can disassociate yourself from what is happening you will be able to think logically about what to do next. People disassociate in different ways: take a mental or physical step back; change your posture; step into your virtual mentor's shoes (see 'Wise words from virtual mentors', Part 2); imagine yourself as a fly on the wall looking down to gain a more objective view of the situation.

Take time out

If you can, take time out and physically remove yourself from the situation, even if it is just taking yourself off to the toilet. This can help you to disassociate yourself and leave your negative emotions behind. If it is possible to go for a short walk this will be even better.

Remind yourself of past successes

If you start to lose your confidence or get into a negative mood, remind yourself of times when you have successfully handled situations or when you have been feeling any of the positive moods that are listed on the Mood Map at the start of Part 4. Remember how good you felt and the strengths you displayed back then that you can access again today.

Actions to take at the end of the day or after a challenging situation

Check in with yourself

As you have done before and during the day, check in with yourself and assess what mood you are in. Even after a good day, it is possible to feel flat or negative without any apparent cause. Rather than let this ruin your evening, do something to change your state so that you can end your day on a positive note, which will set you up for a good night's sleep and the next day.

Debrief in a constructive way

If you are feeling negative about how you handled something or your inner critic is giving you a hard time, make sure that you review what has happened in a constructive way (see 'Debriefing using your wisdom', Part 2).

If necessary, visualise how you would do it differently next time

This can act as a final convincer to yourself and your inner critic that you will be able to cope with the situation again. Do this by looking up and visualising how you will handle it successfully in the future.

Change any negative beliefs that have arisen from the process

As with preparing for your day ahead, you may become aware of negative beliefs that have arisen because of the day's activities that might make it hard to relax and have a good night's sleep. For example: 'I'm useless at doing X,' 'I am never going to be able to change Y,' or 'X situation is never going to change so why bother?'. Do the 'Transforming your beliefs' exercise at the end of Part 4 to assist you in creating more empowering beliefs that will make you feel more positive about yourself, your abilities and the future.

Go ahead and celebrate

You might not want to celebrate every evening (on the other hand…!). But too many people wait until everything is done, dusted and achieved before celebrating. For me, as a great list maker, I like the sense of satisfaction at the end of the day, when I have achieved things. Even if sometimes my day starts to hit the skids, if I am able to turn it around, I can then celebrate the fact that I did. Celebrating does not necessarily mean cracking open a bottle of bubbly; it can be just acknowledging that you've won through despite obstacles, so that you can feel pleased with yourself at the end of the day.

Kick back, switch off

There is always more to do, especially if you listen to your inner critic. More housework, bills to sort, work to do – the list goes on. Make sure that you spend some time each evening just kicking back and switching off in whatever way suits you. Yes, I know some people say ironing is relaxing, but I don't believe them! If you are one of those people who can't switch off unless everything's done – just bear in mind it will never all be done, not until we are dead, and even then we'll probably still have a pile of ironing left to do!

So make sure that you have a number of activities or processes you can draw on to help you to manage your mood and control your inner critic throughout your day.

'Action may not always bring happiness; but there is no happiness without action.'

Benjamin Disraeli

'Chin up!'

Look up to feel more positive

It might sound a bit daft to say that looking up will make you feel better, but there is actually a scientific reason why it does. And we do unconsciously know that looking up rather than looking down makes us feel better as we have expressions like:

'Chin up!' – when we are trying to cheer someone up.
'Down in the dumps' – when we describe feeling low.

If you think about it, when you are happy and walking along the street you tend to look up and around you. When you are feeling down, low or angry, you tend to look down. In order to experience our negative emotions and hear the negative inner dialogue with our inner critic and Fearful Child we naturally and unconsciously look down. However, this can make us feel even worse as we can get into a downward spiral of negative inner dialogue, feeling bad, then more negative thoughts and down it goes.

Why does where we look affect how we feel?

Depending on where we look we access different parts of our brain and this affects how we feel. There are two reasons why when we look up we feel more positive. Firstly, when you look up you access the part of your brain that helps you to visualise the future – you can therefore see beyond your current problems, which tends to have a positive impact on how you feel. Secondly, when you are looking up it is almost impossible to have a negative feeling or thought – if you do your head or your eyes come down to enable you to connect with the part of your brain that allows you to experience negative feelings. So just keep on looking up in order to feel positive and to see a brighter future!

We do this quite naturally when we are feeling confident about ourselves and the situation we are in. If someone asks us a question about something we know, we will usually look up momentarily to access the answer in our brain, then look back to the questioner and answer the question. If we are unsure of ourselves we often look down, we start to feel bad as we don't know the answer, we doubt ourselves, we then engage in destructive inner dialogue with our inner critic and follow the spiral downwards. For example, think about a time when you felt intimidated by someone – maybe during an interview, or talking to your bank manager. You probably started to look down, which puts you on the slippery slope of negative thinking, affecting your thoughts, feelings and your ability to communicate with the other person.

It seems that we naturally look up when we are trying to stop ourselves from crying. Perhaps we don't consciously know why it helps, but unconsciously we know it does. In fact I was telling this to some managers on a course and one of the guys said he had noticed himself looking at the ceiling of the church during his father's funeral to stop himself from crying.

So we naturally, unconsciously look up to help us control our emotions, and at other times end up looking down and losing the battle with our thoughts and mood. Now that you know about this you can take conscious action to use it to manage your mood.

Encourage yourself to look up

Many of my clients have little Post-its on their computers saying 'Look up'. Others position postcards with positive personal memories associated with them high up on their office or home walls. Then when they look up at them it triggers positive memories and emotions.

> **Q.** What can you use as a trigger to remind yourself to look up?

Visualising success

What we visualise has a profound affect on how we feel, and once more the influence of our inner critic is apparent. If when we think about our day ahead – a presentation to be done, a challenging conversation with a family member – we visualise all the things that could go wrong, we are going to feel pretty bad about it. By contrast, if we learn to visualise success and how we can handle potentially difficult situations effectively, we will feel more positive and motivated, and be in a stronger position to fend off our inner critic.

> *'Imagination is more important than knowledge.'*
>
> Albert Einstein

When it comes to understanding the psychology of success there seems to be a lot more research carried out into sport than how we live our lives day to day. However, we can learn from what they have discovered in the field of sport.

One of the findings is that those people who back up their physical practice with visualising the successful completion of a game, shot or race, are more successful than those who only physically rehearse.

Many successful sportspeople spend time visualising their success beforehand and even while travelling to an event. Golfers visualise playing the whole course in their head, runners see, hear and feel themselves running each step in a race, while rugby players visualise getting the ball over the bar or scoring the try. It has been found that when people do this their muscles react and it is like their whole body mentally rehearses successful completion of the event or game.

Visualising success not failure

Unfortunately what we often do, with the help of our nagging inner critic and Fearful Child, is visualise failure and things going wrong. This can turn into a self-fulfilling prophecy, as it affects how we feel, our motivation, how we communicate, our behaviour and the end result of the action we take.

'When you clearly envision the outcome of victory, engrave it upon your heart, and are firmly convinced that you will attain it, your brain makes every effort to realise the mental image you have created. And then through your increasing efforts, that victory is finally made a reality.'

Daisaku Ikeda, speech on 'Our Mental Attitude Changes Everything'

How to go about visualising success

While coaching people through this process I've found that not everyone gets a clear visual image in front of them; others see it in their mind's eye, or feel or hear it. People often think they need to be able to see a vivid movie. However, I encourage people to continue with the process even if they don't appear to be able to visualise anything. Having worked with one client who was not at all a visual person, he found that persisting with this process helped him to visualise how he wanted to handle challenging situations.

As long as you keep on looking up during this exercise (keep your eyes looking up, not just your head) you will be accessing your visual cortex and be in a better position to 'visualise' success.

You might find it useful to read through the following exercise before you do it.

Step 1
Sit or stand depending on what is more comfortable for you and look up to where the wall meets the ceiling in a normal-sized room. Some people find it useful to imagine either a cinema or giant TV screen on the wall and project their visualisations onto it; others don't need to do this.

Step 2
Now start to see yourself in the situation that you find challenging and want to succeed in, or visualise yourself succeeding over a

period of time. You need to make this visualisation as vivid as possible. Make sure it has:

- Colour and moving pictures.
- Clear sound so you can hear yourself (including hearing any positive thoughts or self talk), hear other people, hear other sounds or even music if appropriate.

Step 3
Run through the 'movie' of you being successful in this situation:

- See whatever there is to see – see yourself succeeding, see the positive impact on others.
- Hear whatever there is to hear – hear how you sound when you are succeeding, how confident, clear and strong your voice is; hear other people's positive comments and reactions.
- Feel what it feels like to be successful.
- Notice the positive impact that success has on your thoughts, feelings and behaviour in this situation.

If your mind says 'Yes but what if X happens?' or if you find doubt coming up or your eyes and head coming down, keep on looking up and visualise yourself successfully handling your fears and concerns.

Step 4 (Optional)
When you are completely happy with the vision you have created, secure it with either a physical, visual or auditory anchor – see the next section for details of how to do this.

Practice sets you up for success

The more you use this visualisation process the easier it will become. In the end visualising success will become part of what you do naturally when you are preparing yourself for different situations. The more you do it, the more it will become second nature.

You will start to notice the difference in how you feel when you are visualising and thinking about success, rather than letting your inner critic dwell on your shortcomings and potential failures. You will become more positive, enthusiastic and motivated.

When could you use this visualisation process?

Here are some situations where people have found it useful to visualise success:

- Having planned out the next five years of her life, a friend regularly visualises herself succeeding and completing each stage.
- Before attending an interview a client visualised himself entering the room, facing the interview panel and confidently answering the questions.
- A manager had an appraisal to conduct and he was worried about the individual's reactions, so he visualised how we would handle all possibilities and then was reassured that he could deal with them.
- A client used it to help her prepare for a major presentation so that she felt confident in using the equipment and handling questions. These were two things that she was nervous about, especially if the equipment went wrong. So she visualised herself successfully handling this eventuality.
- A friend facing her first child's first day at school ran through in her mind how she would prepare him the night before, how she wanted the morning to go and how she would occupy herself at home when he was at school.

Make a list of when you could use visualisation to assist you.

Anchors and triggers

All around us there are various things (people, songs, objects, scenes, movies, etc.) that trigger off different memories, thoughts and emotions in us. Many of these will trigger positive emotions and memories, while others will trigger negative emotions in us. The following are just a few things that might trigger an emotional response:

- A song that brings back memories of a particular event or time in your life.
- An advert for a destination that reminds you of a holiday you have spent there.
- Particular words or phrases that act as a 'red flag to a bull' and can distract you and make you feel angry.
- A natural phenomenon such as a rainbow, or a scene of outstanding natural beauty, which reminds you of other beautiful things you have seen in your life.
- Someone mentions a person's name from your past and the thought of that particular person brings a sinking feeling of dread in your stomach.

So around us are many different things we see, hear or even smell and taste that bring back memories with either positive or negative emotions tacked onto them. These can result in a rush of thoughts and feelings, and can arouse your inner critic or Fearful Child and create an unresourceful state. These sights, sounds, smells and tastes act as anchors to positive and negative memories and emotions. When they come into our environment they trigger these emotions.

Getting whammied!

One of my colleagues used to talk about getting 'whammied' by something or someone. This is when something triggers such a negative response and unresourceful state that it feels like getting kicked in the stomach or getting 'knocked sideways'. It is often at these times, when you are distracted and feeling less than confident and centred, that the inner critic can quietly slip in and turn the knife.

Anchors and triggers

Our level of resourcefulness is linked to these positive and negative emotions which are 'anchored' to particular events, activities, songs or places. Your past experiences act as an anchor. Whenever these anchors are seen or heard again they trigger the emotion, whether it is good or bad.

Past experience creates a positive or negative emotion. This is then **anchored** to something associated with that experience.

Days, weeks or years later, that **anchor** is seen, or heard or even smelt and tasted again, **triggering** the positive or negative emotion attached to it.

How does this impact on you?

Day to day
These anchors can trigger different emotions on a day-to-day basis, and you can be at the mercy of your environment, letting your mood be altered by what occurs around you. However, you can set and use your own anchors to help maintain a more positive state of mind.

Particular events
Your negative reactions can be triggered at crucial moments: at a job interview, family gathering, first date or important presentation. Getting 'whammied' at these times can lead you to under-perform or not enjoy the activity. This can serve to reinforce the negative anchor with that experience, setting you up for more failures in the future and providing more fuel for your inner critic. Setting an anchor that you can trigger at these crucial moments will assist you in managing your mood and performing effectively.

Spotting your triggers and the impact on you

What triggers do you have? In what situations does this happen?	What is the impact of this?
Positive triggers:	
Negative triggers:	

Setting your own anchors – triggering positive emotions
To trigger more positive emotions more of the time you can use old positive anchors as well as creating new ones that will help you in particular situations.

When we feel positive about ourselves our inner critic has much less chance of having an impact.

Use the anchors you already have
The first thing to realise is that there are already anchors that trigger positive emotions and it might be about making sure that you have as many of these in your day-to-day environment as possible. My office is full of inspiring quotes, postcards from New Zealand and other beautiful scenes – including a calendar with rainbows that my mum bought me, as she knew I liked them. Every holiday I go on seems to have an associated song or singer that evokes memories of the relaxing, fun times on that particular holiday. When I listen to those songs when I get home they take me right back to those happy times. I find that the more I use and revel in the memories the more powerful the triggers are.

Create new anchors
These can either be anchors for use in daily life or for particular challenging situations. I had a client who was a senior manager and whose mood could easily be swayed by events around her, resulting in very unproductive exchanges with her team. After coaching her she decided to put a particular postcard on her office notice board, high up (see 'Chin up!' earlier in this Part for the significance of this). When she looked at it, it evoked very positive emotions that helped to calm her down and put her in a different mood.

Think about positive anchors that you could have around you: in your bedroom, kitchen, living room, car and office. These could be things you see, hear, touch, smell or taste.

Anchors for challenging times

If you know that the time ahead is going to be challenging either in or out of work, then think about setting and using specific anchors that will uplift and inspire you to keep on going. This could be inspirational quotes or pictures placed where you will see them regularly or using music to enhance your mood. When I was in New Zealand I knew that I was going to come back to challenging times so I bought a journal with wonderful pictures of New Zealand mountains. During the first few weeks they acted as a constant reminder as I wrote in my journal.

Anchors for specific situations

There are times when we are facing potentially challenging situation and we need to be at our best, but feel less than confident. This is when we can set specific anchors to help us feel as positive and confident as possible. A client who does not like cold calling (who does!) has anchored positive inner resources and feelings onto his favourite pen. When he sits down to make the calls and picks the pen up it triggers the positive emotions and helps him feel motivated and confident. The next section will take you through the process of creating anchors for particular inner resources for specific situations.

Check your life for positive triggers

- Make sure that you spend time with friends and people who trigger positive emotions, especially when you are feeling less than positive.
- Check your environment – do you have pictures and objects that are positive triggers and help to make you feel happy, relaxed and positive?
- Have to hand music that evokes positive emotions – have a selection, ones to relax to, energise you and cheer you up.

- Set yourself a positive anchor that you can trigger any place, any time to feel more confident, positive and able to cope with life's challenges and to fight off your inner critic.

Inner resources

There are many philosophies and theories that say that we have all the resources we need inside ourselves to cope with and thrive in life, it is just that we often fail to recognise this fact and tap into these inner resources. The thirteenth-century Buddhist Nichiren Daishonin said that the only difference between a common mortal and a Buddha is that the latter is awakened to the fact that they are a Buddha and that they have enormous potential, while a common mortal does not see their own Buddhahood or innate potential.

In neurolinguistic programming, or NLP, it is also believed that people have all the resources necessary within them, it is just that they either do not realise this or cannot access these positive resources at the times when they need them most.

'I was always looking outside myself for strength and confidence but it comes from within. It is there all the time.'

Anna Freud

What do we mean by inner resources?
Inner resources can be many things, many qualities that human beings possess, such as:

Courage
Humour
Light-heartedness
Patience
Contentment
Not taking things personally

Confidence
Wisdom
Energy/life force
Trustworthiness
Ability to step back/take a deep breath
Optimism
Clear-headedness/clear thinking
Sense of perspective
Compassion
Perseverance
Persistence
Assertiveness
Pragmatism
Focus/drive

All these qualities are within us and at some time or another we have used them or seen glimpses of them. We can bring these resources into play right now and in the future whenever we need them.

Your inner resources

Look at the above list and tick the qualities that you have experienced in yourself over the last month. While you are doing this, your inner critic might step in and say 'Hey, you can't tick patience as you got impatient in the queue at the supermarket last week,' or 'You gave up learning French,' or 'You were scared about doing that presentation at work.' Ignore what the inner critic says, as you know that despite the times when you have felt less than resourceful, there will have been many occasions where you have demonstrated many of these qualities.

Q. What are your top six qualities that you are most proud of in yourself?

Failure to recognise these qualities in ourselves

There can be a number of reasons why we fail to recognise these qualities in ourselves, one of which is that our inner critic dismisses our successes and only focuses on the times when we have failed to bring these qualities to the fore.

Another reason is that people can misunderstand what these qualities really mean in practice. Take courage, for example. People often say to me that they are not courageous because they experience fear. However, you will be pleased to know that the dictionary defines courage as 'going ahead despite fear'. If, for example, the thought of speaking to groups of people brings up no fears then it actually requires no courage. Whereas if going into a room of strangers at a party brings up lots of fear then it requires a lot more courage.

The same is true with perseverance – there is a belief that people who persevere never have moments of doubt or moments when they feel they are moving backwards. This is not true: the essence of perseverance is to keep going despite these doubts and set-backs. But our inner critic would like us to believe otherwise.

Other people's perspectives

It can be useful to ask a trusted friend to pick out which of the qualities listed on the previous page sum you up. If your inner critic disagrees with their assessment ask them for examples as to why they chose those qualities. You might find it quite illuminating.

Moving to a resourcefulness state – you can do it!

We often find ourselves naturally moving from a neutral or happy state to an unhappy and unresourceful one in response to triggers in our environment, reactions to what other people say or do, or in response to our own inner critic. However, we can also move from unresourceful states to ones of resourcefulness. We have the choice and power to do this right now. We do not have to stay stuck with our negative emotions. For example, if we are angry about something it is far better to change state to one that will assist us in assertively, rather than aggressively, dealing with the situation.

Accessing your inner resources

As we are only common mortals we sometimes lose sight of these great qualities within us. However, there are exercises you can do to resource yourself and access all the inner resources you need to help you in a particular situation or in life.

Seven steps to anchoring resourcefulness

You can use this exercise to resource yourself either for a specific situation that is coming up (e.g. a potentially challenging conversation with your boss or a family member, or a stressful time meeting a deadline) or as a general resource to help you in your day-to-day life when things start to become difficult.

Although the following exercise may appear lengthy it can actually be done in a few minutes once you are used to doing it. This can be before you set off for work or when preparing yourself for a difficult situation.

Step 1: Create an anchor

Your anchor can be anything that you can call upon quickly and unobtrusively. It could be:

- An action like putting your thumb and little finger together – it needs to be something that you don't usually do so that you do not trigger it accidentally.
- Something you can touch, e.g. your watch, a ring.
- A word you see or hear in your head.

- A song you hear in your head that is significant for you.
- A colour or even picture that you see in your mind's eye.

Step 2: Select your resources
Now think of three qualities that would be useful to draw upon in the situation you are facing or in daily life. You might want to refer back to the list of qualities to assist you in doing this.

Step 3: Connect with the positive power of these resources
Think of the first resource and go back to a time when you have used it or drawn upon it (this could be in or out of work). Think of yourself back in the situation when you were using this resource. Fully immerse yourself in the situation: see what there is to see, hear what there is to hear and feel what it felt like to use this positive inner resource and the positive impact it had on your thoughts, feelings and behaviour. Once you are fully immersed in the positive sights, sounds and feelings associated with this resource and experience, trigger your anchor so that this resource is anchored to it. Once it is anchored you can let go of the anchor.

Step 4: Visualise the future and anchor your resources
Look up to where the wall meets the ceiling and imagine yourself using this resource in the future in situations which you might find challenging. Imagine yourself in this challenging situation using this inner resource. Notice the positive impact that it has on your thoughts, feelings and behaviour in this situation. When you are completely happy with the vision you have, anchor it with your sight, sound or physical anchor.

Step 5
Now think of your second inner resource and go through Steps 3 and 4 again.

Step 6
Now think of your third inner resource and go through steps 3 and 4 again. Once you have anchored all three inner resources, look up again and visualise yourself using all three resources together to create a really resourceful and successful future. Once you are entirely satisfied with the positive vision you have of the future, anchor it for the final time.

Step 7: Trigger your resources in the future
Either just before or when you are faced with a challenging situation trigger your positive resources by firing the anchor: hearing the song or word, seeing the picture, using the physical anchor. In this way you will access the positive resources that will counteract the effect of the negative anchors in your environment.

A shortcut to resourcefulness
If you are not in the position to do this whole exercise then you can simply think of three resources that would help you in the situation you are either in or about to enter and imagine yourself using those resources in that situation. I remember a time when I was driving to see a client to conduct a potentially tricky meeting between two managers who were not getting on with each other. I became aware that I was in a less than resourceful state. I thought of three resources that would assist me and I felt much more prepared, knowing that I could trust my abilities, rather than panicking about how I was going to handle the meeting.

Increasing your resourcefulness

- Build up a bank of inner resources and anchors that you can easily and quickly draw on in different situations.
- Spot when you are feeling in a less than positive and resourceful state and draw on the resources you have created during this exercise.

- Use the quick shortcut resourcing process if you do not have time or space to do the whole thing.
- Recognise that you do not have to remain in an unresourceful state: it is within your power to change this right now and create a more positive and empowering state to be in.

Questions to transform your mood

When we are in a negative mood it is easy to be swamped by the emotions associated with it and it becomes difficult to think logically and deal with the situation effectively.

One technique for transforming negative moods is to pose questions to yourself that will change your mindset.

Over the years I have found that focussing on a few of the following questions can help me move through my mood and onto a more positive place. You will find that one or two of the questions will be most suitable for transforming your mood. So play around with them and see which questions best suit you. Sometimes it is not the most obvious ones. I remember being in a very dark mood and facing a very challenging situation. Working through the exercise, I came to 'How can you deal with this and still have fun?' At first I thought this was ridiculous – how could I possibly have fun when I was facing this situation and in this state? But it got me thinking whether this was possible. Which of course it is, if you actually take the question seriously and apply yourself to finding a way. It certainly changed my mood and changed my beliefs around this whole topic.

Pick a situation – pick a question

Think of a situation you are facing or have faced which creates a negative and unhelpful mood in you. Practise using some of the questions below and notice how your mood and thoughts about the situation change:

- How long are you going to let this mood or situation get to you?
- Can you find a fun way of dealing with this?
- If you did not have this problem, how would you feel right now? What would you do?
- What three things or inner resources can help you in this situation?
- How can you deal with this and still have fun or enjoy yourself?
- How will you view this in a week, month or year's time?
- What would happen if you dropped this mood right now?
- What has this situation got to teach you, what can you learn from it?
- How would X deal with this? (A friend, colleague or mentor)
- How can you send this mood on its way?
- If this mood was a colour/animal/cartoon character what would it be?
- How can you take the sting out of this situation?

Why do these questions help?

What these questions do is engage either your Adult self or, in some cases, your creative Fun Child. They make you stand back, be more objective about a situation. They help you to move out of the Emotional, Fearful or Angry Child or Critical Parent mode and enable you to think logically and move on.

> 'Choice is the crown of life. Not to choose, is not to be alive... Choose joy and follow after it.'
>
> Brian Keenan

Mastering your mind

This section is about mastering your mind so that your thoughts will support you in what you want to do in life. If we fail to do this it is easy to find ourselves in a spiral of negative thinking and much easier for our inner critic to chip in and further undermine our confidence. Our thoughts affect how we feel and in turn impact on our behaviour. Therefore one way to manage our mood is to start to master our minds.

By changing the way we think we will become stronger, our inner critic will find fewer chinks in our armour to aim at and we will increase our chances of success in situations and in life in general.

Pink hippos

Let's do a little experiment. For a moment I need you to make sure that whatever you do, you do not think about a pink hippo floating in the air in front of you wearing a blue tutu, a green feather boa and a yellow hat.

What happened? Did you see the pink hippo even though I said don't think about it?

Two things happened here. Firstly your brain is very obedient and tends to do what you tell it to do – so watch out what you say to it. Secondly, your brain cannot process negatives. In order to understand what it is not meant to do, your brain has to imagine doing it and by the time that it has done that it has forgotten it was not meant to! Think about when you say to yourself or someone else:

'Don't forget to post the letter.'
'Don't slip.'
'Don't get stressed out about the presentation.'
'Stop criticising yourself.'

Your mind starts to imagine you doing this, and before you know it you've slipped, feel more stressed and so forth. Now if this is something you want to do then this is fine. But if you are wanting to be calm before a presentation or you want to start praising yourself and being more positive, you need to tell yourself this in positive terms:

'I must remember to post this letter when I go past the post box.'
'I must walk carefully and safely here.' (I use this a lot when out walking on my own on difficult terrain)
'I want to stay calm and relaxed before and during this presentation.'
'I want to acknowledge my strengths and achievements and feel good about myself.'

As with visualising success, when you say something to yourself (or to others) in a positive way your brain starts to imagine it, your body tries it on for size and you set up the patterns of positive thought that will allow the behaviour to follow.

Transforming pink hippo thoughts
Write a list of things that you want to change or do differently (e.g. I want to stop losing my temper).
Are you thinking about them in positive terms?
If not, then reword them in a positive way (e.g. I want to stay calm and rational).

Our inner critic and pink hippos
As our inner critic is so negative and provides a constant barrage of criticism about ourselves and our lives, it is easy to get into

the habit of wording things in the negative and being less than optimistic about ourselves and things we want to change. Our thoughts affect our mood, how we feel and how we behave. Therefore to start to manage your mood and your inner critic you have to take control of your thoughts and how you phrase things when you are speaking to yourself and others.

The more positive we are in both our mind and what we say the more confident, enthusiastic and determined we will feel. As our feelings affect our behaviour we will be in a better position to act positively and succeed in what we are doing.

What's important isn't always marked 'Urgent'...

Dodgy logic and wonky thinking

As I wrote this book I came to realise that the inner critic often makes us suffer from what I now call 'dodgy logic' or 'wonky thinking'. If you have spoken your inner critic-driven thoughts out loud to someone else, you will probably have noticed how illogical and off the mark they sounded. But while they remain in your head, going around and around, you can believe them to be true.

Get it out into the open

I have found that when I have shared some of my dodgy logic with my friends, they were very quick to point out the ridiculousness of what I was thinking, in a kind, supportive manner – or by laughing out loud!

Sometimes as I spoke I would be able to identify that the words were coming from my inner critic rather than my inner wisdom.

Another good way of moving out of a destructive cycle of wonky thinking is by writing these thoughts down. I will often write out my thoughts in my journal and quite quickly I can see how wonky my thinking is and then bring in my wise self to gain a different perspective on the situation.

Dodgy logic and old beliefs

Dodgy logic is usually based on old beliefs that are no longer relevant to you and your life today – and perhaps they never were.

You might want to think about any old beliefs that no longer serve you and may feed your dodgy logic. For example: 'I must be perfect, I must not make a mistake,' 'I must please everyone,' 'I must not show my feelings.'

The 'Transforming your beliefs' exercise at the end of this Part can be used to transform any unhelpful beliefs that are hindering you in life into more constructive, positive and empowering beliefs.

Creating empowering beliefs

The inner critic is based on a set of beliefs about what is right and wrong with you and the world. These beliefs might have been created as a result of past experiences or might have been inherited from our families and other significant people as we were growing up. Many of the beliefs that we have are positive, helpful and relevant to who we are today and the world that we live in, while others might no longer be appropriate (if they ever were) or are destructive, disempowering, hold us back and create unhappiness.

The process of creating and changing beliefs happens the whole time quite naturally and unconsciously. Maybe we have held a belief for a long time and then someone says or does something or something happens in the world that shows us it is not true. We might change our initial belief, but what sometimes happens is that we ignore the evidence and hang onto our old beliefs.

The impact of our beliefs on our lives

We might be aware of some broad beliefs and that they impact on our daily behaviour:

It is wrong to steal or cheat.
Do unto others as you would like to be done unto you.
What goes around, comes around.

For example, one day when I was food shopping I went to put my bags in the boot of my car and discovered some earrings I had put in the trolley, which had not gone through the till. They only cost three pounds and I could easily have driven away without paying for them. But my beliefs about it being wrong to steal, as well as the belief that we reap the results of the causes we make, impelled me to go back into the supermarket and pay for them. So our daily actions are influenced by these beliefs.

In fact we have a whole maze of beliefs stored in our mind, that moment by moment have an impact on how we approach our life. Many of these we are not even conscious of. Often when I am coaching clients they start off the process being pretty much unaware of how their beliefs are affecting their thoughts, feelings and behaviour. It is only when someone like a coach or good friend asks you questions about your behaviour or what is stopping you doing things that you to become aware of your thoughts, which are driven by your beliefs. These beliefs also affect our feelings, which then impact on our behaviour and how successful we are in different situations and in life.

Changing beliefs in order to change behaviour

As our beliefs have such a strong impact on our behaviour, if we want to change a piece of behaviour it can be helpful to explore the beliefs connected with it, which can either be driving the behaviour or hindering us in changing. I remember watching a demonstration on a course I was attending with a man who wanted to give up smoking. When the trainer started to explore his beliefs around smoking, which he had been doing since he was 15, he said that smoking was cool, it showed his rebellious nature. So although he wanted to give up smoking, he realised he still wanted to feel cool and rebellious and he associated smoking with this. Until he transformed his beliefs he was probably going to find it hard to stop smoking and had in fact found it impossible up until that moment.

Q. What behaviour do you want to change?

Q. What beliefs do you have around this that might hinder you changing?

Q. What beliefs do you have around this that might help you to change?

Are beliefs positive or negative?

This is a question that I have posed to myself while writing this section. Beliefs are a matter of opinion – who am I or you to judge whether they are good or bad? What is probably more useful is to explore the impact that they have on different aspects of your life. Do your beliefs help or hinder you in what you want to do with your life? Do they help or hinder you in being healthy and happy?

The criticisms that our inner critics throw at us are usually based on beliefs that will hinder progress and happiness. For example, 'You get what you deserve': if you believe this your inner critic is probably going to have a field day whenever something goes wrong in your life, and not help you to learn and deal with the problems that come along. Other beliefs enable us to behave in a positive, constructive way in whatever area of our lives they relate to.

Clusters of beliefs

Usually beliefs come in clusters around particular topics. We tend to have a range of beliefs around money, relationships, parenthood, war, peace, education – you name it, we have beliefs around it. These beliefs will either help or hinder us in being happy and successful in these areas.

What tends to happen is that if you can tackle one of the beliefs associated with a topic the others will also be transformed.

For example, a person might have the following beliefs around money: 'Both too much or too little money causes problems'; 'I'm hopeless with money'; 'If you have too much money then you can't tell who your real friends are' (which says something about their beliefs on friendships as well); 'To get enough money I would have to work as hard as my dad and be dead from a heart attack at 50'. As you can imagine these beliefs are likely to hinder the person in their financial matters.

By contrast, someone with the following beliefs about money might feel more positive about their financial situation, whatever it is: 'There is more than enough money in the world for everyone'; 'I'm learning a lot about money and how to manage it and there are always other people I can call on for advice'; 'I am happy whatever my level of income, it does not affect my state of mind'; 'I'm a resourceful person and can always find new ways of earning money'.

Think about your beliefs relating to the following areas of life and write them down: marriage, parenting, money, health and illness, happiness.

Now, think about the beliefs you have just written down and whether they help or hinder you to be successful and happy in these areas of your life.

Illogical beliefs

Beliefs are frequently illogical. Even when presented with substantial evidence to the contrary, we still hang onto our beliefs. I remember a time when coaching a client who was nervous about asking for a pay rise. A colleague had tried to reassure her that she was great at negotiating, had exceeded her targets and would have no problems, having done this loads of times before. Even though all the evidence pointed logically to the fact that she should have been confident, she wasn't. During the coaching session it became clear that the reason for this came down to her beliefs about asking for more money, which were 'Why should I deserve more when everyone has worked hard this year?' and 'What if my boss says no, will it adversely affect my working relationship with them?'. Once she had identified what was really concerning her we were able to work on transforming these beliefs to support her in asking for her pay rise.

We all have illogical beliefs and you might want to take a look at the ones you wrote down in the previous exercise to see if any of them seem to be illogical and not based on fact.

Beliefs and our life's journey

I had a friend who believed that all men were either wimps or bastards, a belief that horrified me at the time. Firstly, I knew many men who were neither and felt aggrieved on their behalf. Secondly, I knew she was not interested in the wimps and therefore was continually being hurt by the so-called 'bastards' she dated, not knowing that there was a middle option. Also, this belief stopped her from building supportive and constructive relationships. So how can we ensure that our beliefs have a positive impact on our life's journey and lead us to make constructive decisions and lead happy and fulfilled lives?

Creating positive and helpful thoughts and beliefs

Our beliefs about a situation, other people or ourselves can be either positive and helpful or negative and limiting. What you think and the beliefs you have will show in some way when you communicate with others. It will either be in your tone of voice, your body language or the words you use. It is therefore important to check that your beliefs and thoughts are positive and going to help you in the situation you are in. As Henry Ford said:

'Whether you think you can or you think you can't, you're absolutely right!'

Think about a situation that you find challenging.
Now think about all the beliefs that you have about it and categorise them into empowering or limiting beliefs.
What is the impact of the empowering beliefs on how I feel and behave?
What is the impact of the limiting beliefs on how I feel and behave?

Transforming your beliefs

The following exercise will help you to transform unhelpful, limiting beliefs into positive, empowering ones. It will involve you standing up and moving around, as this frees up the mind and enables you to literally step out of the negative into the positive.

Step 1

Stand where you have space to move around both in front of you and to your right. Now step forward into your negative belief and say what it is (often it is different from the one you thought of when you were sitting down). Notice how this makes you feel, whether you have any pictures or words associated with it in your mind's eye.

Step 2

Step out of the negative belief and walk about three paces to your right and then step forward. Ask yourself 'What might be a more empowering belief?' Say what it is. Notice how this feels, whether there are any new pictures or words associated with it. See, hear and feel yourself living this more empowering belief.

Step 3

If you do not feel 100 per cent positive or certain about the new belief helping you in the future, take another step to your right and then step forward. Ask yourself 'What might be an *even more* empowering belief?' Say what it is. Notice how this feels, whether there are any new pictures or words associated with it.

Step 4

Stay in the positive belief and look up, roughly where the wall meets the ceiling. Imagine yourself living this belief. Visualise a cinema screen and play a movie of you living this belief. Make sure that it is in colour with moving pictures and sound. See, hear and feel what it is like. Play different versions of you living the belief in different situations until you are fully experiencing what life is like with this belief.

Step 5
Anchor the belief so that you can easily access it on other occasions for more on the anchoring process see 'Seven steps to anchoring resourcefulness' earlier in this Part.

Reap the benefits of changing beliefs
When you transform your beliefs you will notice that you feel lighter (without the negative beliefs weighing you down), more motivated and ready to move forward.

The previous exercise is one that I use on a regular basis whenever I become aware of a negative belief lurking around that I need to replace with a more empowering one. My clients who use it find that by creating more positive and helpful beliefs they end up feeling more positive and motivated.

'Aerodynamically the bumble bee shouldn't be able to fly, but the bumble bee doesn't know it, so it goes on flying anyway.'
Mary Kay Ash

Part 5

Supporting Yourself

'Learn to distinguish between straining and stretching yourself – the former leads to injury, the latter to development.'

Anne Dickson

This Part is about caring for and supporting ourselves. After a lifetime of undermining ourselves and beating ourselves up, it may be something that we need to start to do for the first time. It is about understanding the difference between self care and being selfish, learning to ask for support, and knowing how to look after yourself, as well as learning how to be proud of your achievements and realising that you deserve the best.

How much do you support yourself?

Part of mastering your inner critic is ensuring that you support yourself physically, emotionally, socially, mentally and spiritually. This is important as the inner critic undermines us and one way to counteract it is to actively support ourselves. The following questions will help you to think through what you do to support yourself.

Think about your daily life...	Always	Some-times	Rarely	Never
Are you able to turn to friends and colleagues for support?				
Do you forgive and support yourself when you make mistakes?				
Do you take time out to support, nurture or pamper yourself?				
Are you able to ask for help and support before you get overwhelmed?				
Do you appreciate your own strengths and achievements?				
Are you able to let yourself have fun and enjoy life regardless of the challenges you face?				
Do you take action on a daily and weekly basis to support yourself?				

Your responses

Where you have ticked 'Never' or 'Rarely' this provides you with information as to what areas to focus on as you read this section. If you have ticked 'Sometimes' for some items you might want to consider whether the situations concerned have a big enough impact to warrant bearing these in mind as well.

Research shows that people who use a range of supports are better able to deal with pressure and stress in life. As our inner critic will often kick in when we are feeling under pressure or low, the more we support ourselves, the harder it is for the inner critic to take hold and undermine our confidence, satisfaction and happiness.

Self care versus selfishness

What does this mean?

I remember when I was growing up hearing people describing others as being selfish. However, it was never very clear to me why some people's behaviour was labelled as selfish and others' not. The inner critic can be very good at criticising us when we are attempting to care for ourselves. Society or those around us can often provide it with ammunition about being selfish, because of a lack of understanding of what self care means, the benefits of it and how it differs from selfishness.

Interestingly, the dictionary has no listing for 'self care', although 'selfishness', 'self love' and 'selfless' are covered. But these words describe the extremes, from being narcissistic and only caring for ourselves, to having no concern for our own health and happiness. What I aim to do, and would encourage others to do, is to practise 'self care' as an antidote to always undermining ourselves or ignoring our needs while supporting and giving to others.

So how do we make sure that we care for ourselves, as well as caring for others? This is crucial as our inner critic can drive us to take care of others and support them while neglecting ourselves.

Giving to yourself and others

Over the last few years I have discovered that I am in a much better position to give to others if I make sure that I also give to myself, especially if I have to support others over a long period of time. Although this might seem obvious, many people seem to forgo their own needs when supporting others. Their thinking goes something like this:

'How can I think about myself when there is so much to do or X to care for?'

'I have not got time to pamper myself.'

'When this is over then I will do X, Y and Z to look after myself.'

But if you do not look after yourself, by the time you've supported others, you are either ill, miserable or have even forgotten how to look after yourself. This also affects your ability to care for others, as you are likely to have less patience, be more irritable and less compassionate towards others and less able to make wise decisions, all of which will impact on the quality of care you provide to others.

'You're selfish'

What if someone labels us as selfish when we want to fulfil our own needs? Their comments can feed into our inner critic and our Fearful Child, making us feel bad. However, rather than assuming that your inner (and the outer) critic are correct you might want to first of all consider another perspective: is that individual able to ask for their needs to be fulfilled? Some people call others selfish when they are used to giving to others, but not good at making sure that their own needs are met. Therefore, they tend to label people who are able to ask for their needs to be fulfilled as selfish, rather than stop and find out how they do it and learn how to do it for themselves.

One response can be to ask whether they need any support or help in understanding how they can engage in self care as well, and to encourage them to express their own needs and desires.

In its extreme form, selflessness can become martyrdom. I have certainly witnessed people who, while being selfless in their care of others (whether this is their children, elderly parents, partners or team members), forget about supporting themselves and slip into martyrdom. In the end neither they nor the people they are supporting are happy within this scenario. It usually ends with bitterness on one or both sides of the equation.

In order to care for others in a way that is supportive and healthy for both you and them, it is essential to care for yourself at the same time and base any action on wisdom so it is more likely to benefit both the giver and the receiver.

By controlling our inner critic and using our wisdom we can make the right choices when it comes to supporting ourselves and others.

Parents' versus children's needs

Too often I have seen friends who are busy meeting the needs of their children so that their children are happy, but forgetting about themselves. I have also seen health, sanity and marriages sent into crisis by the parents' lack of self care. Of course we want children to be happy, but I also hear time and again from parents saying that when they are happy and relaxed, their children are more likely to be as well.

Go ahead take some time out

We can end up thinking that there is no way we can take a moment out of caring for others to focus on our needs. We can think that the world will fall apart, our working and home lives won't function without us. However, the reality is that they will, and if we take time out, even an hour or two, then we and others will reap the benefits.

What constitutes self caring for you?

For me it might be:

- Having some 'timeless time' where there are no demands on me for a weekend, a day, half-day, an evening or a couple of hours.
- Going to the cinema – especially on a mid-week afternoon.
- Spending time with a good friend.
- A massage or hugs – it is so important that we experience the power of touch.
- A candlelit bath.
- Delicious things to eat.
- Just sitting and reading the Sunday papers.
- Relaxing and reading a book.
- Buying beautiful journals to write in.
- Having my monthly coaching calls.

Ideally have some things that you can do for yourself so you are not dependent on others for nurturing and pampering.

Q. What do you or can you do to care for yourself?

How to create the space for self care

For some people, especially if they have children, it can feel impossible to indulge themselves, because of a lack of time and/ or money. Some of the following ideas may help:

Create the time and space

If you have children, agree with a friend or family member to look after each other's children for a day, evening or overnight on a monthly or quarterly basis to provide you with time to indulge.

Or find a willing childless friend who would like some fun time with your children and would be willing to kid sit – believe it or not they will enjoy the time alone with the children.

If you don't have children it can still sometimes be a challenge to find time and space to support yourself. You might find that work encroaches on your time or that people expect you to have more time on your hands because you don't have children and therefore expect more of you! Also from my experience I find that most of my friends have children and are busy with them, so unless I am proactive I don't get a look in. However, they always respond positively if I suggest some fun or mutually supportive activities.

Indulgence on a budget
Think about at-home indulgences: curling up with a book and hot chocolate with no one to disturb you; creating your own spa treatments; relaxing in the garden with a glass of wine rather than feeling you need to do the gardening; having a marathon movie afternoon.

Time away from home
Find a friend who lives in a different town (or even country if you are lucky) who would also like time away and house swap. It is a great, inexpensive way to get time away from home.

Fear of indulgence
I wonder if we are still influenced by the old Protestant work ethic that we can't rest and enjoy ourselves until all the work has been done? There will always be more to do: more work, more ironing, more phone calls to make. However, taking time out to relax and care for ourselves will refresh us and give us the energy and motivation to get back to our tasks with renewed vigour.

Asking for support

Do you know what kind of support you need? What stops you from asking for it?

It is good when others offer support, especially if it is what you want, or if they ask you what support you need and are prepared to meet those needs, even if it does not fit into their expectation of support. For example, a fellow Buddhist was going through a very challenging time. When I asked her if there was any support I could offer she said, 'I know it might sound daft, but can you take me to the coach station next week when I get my flight back to the US?' It sounded a reasonable request to me, although not one I could have predicted. And that is the thing: we can't always second guess what support people actually need and they can't guess our needs either.

As people often don't want to interfere they often don't end up offering support. This means that you may well be in a situation where you need to ask for help, whatever that might be. Be specific about what you need and how it will help you in a clear, non-emotional way – so that people do not feel manipulated. Ask with the acceptance that they have a right to say they can't help or not now.

Too independent for your own good

I've noticed that some people are too independent for their own good. Yes, it is great to be able to stand alone, but I now believe it is a sign of strength to know when to ask for support. However, in the past my inner critic would have definitely said, 'You're a wimp, why can't you cope on your own?'

Because our inner critic drives us on we can get to the point where we only 'give in' and ask for support when we are completely laid low. It can also be the control freak in each of us that stops us from allowing others to do things for us, as they won't do it how we would.

Mind reading

> *'The longer you take to say something that needs to be said, the shorter the tone can be when you finally get around to saying it.'*
>
> Peter Karsten

People are not mind readers and cannot always second guess what you need, even if they live with you. So, the more direct and specific you are the more likely you are to have your needs fulfilled.

The quote above really resonates with me. Here it equally applies to asking for help. If you sit there waiting for support, not saying anything, you will end up feeling resentful and seething about not getting the help you need. Then, when you do say something, it will not come out in a clear, constructive and assertive way and probably will lead into a downward spiral of resentment.

Some people say that if their partner, parent or child really loved and cared for them, they should know what to do to support them. From my experience, people are rarely that good at reading minds and can often end up providing no support as they think you are coping, or offering the wrong kind of support. A more constructive approach is to openly discuss what support you all need, which is likely to be very different for each of you. One person might just want to be listened to, someone else might want practical support; another might want to be able to have a laugh at the end of a hard day or some space to be alone. If we asked and listened to each other we might then learn to support each other in appropriate ways.

What stops you from asking for support?
More often than not it will be our inner critic saying things like:

'You should be able to cope without help.'
'Don't be such a wimp.'

'Do you expect everyone to run around after you?
'You'll make people feel guilty if you ask and they can't do it.'
'They are too busy.'
'Don't be so selfish.'

Working on mastering your inner critic will assist you in asking for appropriate support. Firstly, you will become more aware of what support you actually need and secondly, you'll have the confidence to ask for it in a way that will be comfortable for both you and the other person.

Remember: if they can't provide the support you ask for right away, it doesn't mean they won't be able to at another time. And in the meantime you can always resort to some self care and nurturing to keep you going.

Pacing yourself

Have you ever tried to cheer up someone who is feeling low, or has someone tried to pull you out of a low mood? What happened? Did you just dig your heels in even more?

The attempts of others to cheer us up frequently send us even deeper into ourselves and our misery. My friend Peter used to bounce into my office or home full of the joys of life and attempt to jolly me along. His enthusiasm for life and positive outlook just made me feel even more depressed and helpless as I felt I could never be like him. You might have had this kind of experience.

You might also find yourself around people who do the old 'pull yourself together, look at all the things you've got to feel thankful for' routine, which is likely to feed into your inner critic and trigger your Fearful Child. Although there might be an element of truth in this statement, if we are genuinely low or depressed being told this often sends us down further. We probably already know this and are giving ourselves a hard time about not being grateful for what we have. Our inner critics often tell us to:

'Stop moping!'
'Pull yourself together!'
'Count your blessings!'
'Consider yourself lucky!'
'Stop being a wimp!'

So, how can we encourage ourselves to move forward and take action at a pace of life which will suit us, without resorting to bullying techniques?

Pace yourself

Coaches and trainers often talk about pacing the people they are working with. This is about going to where their client is first of all and being there with them until they feel listened to, understood and ready to move forward. By doing this and pacing their clients they can gradually help them to move to a more positive place. It's a lot like training to run a marathon: a runner starts off running for a few minutes every day, and paces themselves, increasing this gradually until they move forward in their fitness.

You can also pace yourself. If you are feeling really low physically, emotionally, mentally or spiritually you might need to allow yourself to be in that place first before moving. There may be a very good reason why you are there that you need to examine before you can move forward.

If you are physically ill you may need to rest and recuperate. If you are mentally exhausted you may need time to recharge your mental batteries. If you are emotionally or spiritually low, feeling angry or anxious, you may need to be with those emotions, learn what you need to learn from them, before you can move on.

Listen to yourself

This is where some compassionate listening to yourself comes in to assist you in that low, angry or anxious place. Listening to your inner thoughts and feelings and acknowledging them will help you to move forward. These thoughts and feelings can be drowned out by your inner critic, which, although it might have a positive intention in wanting you to move forward, usually does not go about it in a constructive and motivating way.

Instead of bullying yourself you can tap into your inner wisdom, which will enable you to make wise decisions as to what you need to do, depending on the circumstances you find yourself in.

How do you pace yourself?

Think about times when you have been physically, emotionally, spiritually or mentally low (and maybe the inner critic has started to nag you). What did you do, or could you have done, to pace yourself?

Different activities will help you to take stock and move on in a more positive way, depending on whether you are physically, mentally, emotionally or spiritually low:

- Physically – napping, taking a relaxing bath, going for a gentle walk, getting some fresh air, having a massage.
- Mentally – doing something that helps you to switch off or recharge your mental energy. Sometimes this can be about doing something energetic – even walking helps because it enables your right and left hemispheres to connect and you will get new insights and inspiration after a walk. Or something that just allows your brain to switch off: reading fiction, watching some TV, any activities that help you to clear your mind.
- Emotionally – talking to a good friend, coach or counsellor, writing in a journal, having a good cry – anything that nurtures you in some way.

• Spiritually – going for walks, listening to music, meditating, exploring art – whatever raises your spirits.

It is about pacing and giving yourself some time and space to deal with things rather than rushing on to the next activity.

Go where the energy is

I am reminded of a comment made by a colleague of mine. We were talking on the phone about the challenges we were facing at the time and he talked about 'going where the energy is'. At the time it was something that I did not do, as my inner critic would always urge me to stick with something even if the energy was not there. Going with your energy is an integral part of pacing yourself. Your inner critic will tell you that you *must* stay with the task in hand, or that you *should* do X and Y even if you don't feel up to it at the time. But if you're struggling with something, it's much wiser to take a break from it and apply yourself to something that better suits your mood, rather than wasting energy by forcing yourself to carry on.

Q. Have there been times in the past when 'going where the energy is' would have helped to move you on, helped you to achieve more?

'Life is so short, we should all move more slowly.'

Thich Nhat Hanh

Caring for your Fearful Child

Many adults don't want to consider the fact that they still have a child inside them, even though their reactions to some events and their behaviour indicate that they are acting in a less than adult way.

While most people are ready to accept that they might have the Fun Child within them, or even the Rebellious or Sulky Child if they are prone to that, it can be harder to own up to the Fearful Child, especially as our inner critic usually thinks that the Fearful Child is being silly and pathetic.

What triggers the Fearful Child?

Having mastered my inner critic and learned how to support myself, most of the time my Fearful Child is well looked after and does not get triggered by things around me. However, there is an MD of a client organisation – a lovely guy who I get on very well with – who will occasionally ask me if I have read a certain management book or heard of a particular model. For some reason, this triggers my Fearful Child and I get a sinking feeling in my stomach. I am back to how I was as a young consultant with the ridiculous notion that if I was a truly professional consultant I would know everything. My Fearful Child thinks I will get 'found out'. Meanwhile in other circumstances if someone asks me if I have heard of a book and I have not, I simply say no and ask them questions about it.

Rational and irrational fears

What are your fears? What situations send you into a fearful state? Our Fearful Child often has lots of different things it is frightened of. Some of our fears appear to be rational to some people, but might appear irrational to others. For example: fear of doing presentations, fear of asking for a pay rise, fear of going to the dentist, fear of flying, spiders, birds – the list goes on. The inner critic can have a field day with our irrational fears. It is therefore important to be able to look after your Fearful Child and his or her fears if you are either going to cope with them or face them squarely and overcome them.

How to support your Fearful Child and even overcome your fears

Listen to yourself
Being compassionate towards yourself and listening to the different parts of yourself that might be in conflict will assist you in overcoming your fears. Listen to what your Fearful Child has to say, rather than let your inner critic walk all over your fears. Remember to bring in your Nurturing Parent and Adult self to assist the Fearful Child in dealing with its fears. If you don't do this then the part of you that you are ignoring will tend to start to shout louder or act up, or you will only hear your inner critic as it is bossier than the other parts of you.

Create a positive outcome in your head
As your Fearful Child focuses on what might go wrong and on 'worst possible scenarios', creating a positive outcome in your head can be one way to counteract this tendency. By creating a positive outcome to work towards in a particular situation, I feel more confident, motivated and courageous. Once you have created a positive outcome, visualise it happening. I can't emphasise enough how important visualising positive outcomes is. The more you visualise something the more your brain and body try it on for size and work out how it will happen.

Resource yourself
The Fearful Child often does not feel equipped to deal with situations that it fears. As a child this might have been true,

especially if the adults in your life did not help you to develop the inner resources and confidence to deal with these situations. Or it might be that we have had a particularly bad experience that knocks our confidence, resulting in our Fearful Child still feeling unable to cope. I was actually fine with dentists as a child, even though I had lots of fillings, but when I was about 13 or 14, a dentist had to take a mould of my mouth which seemed too big for my mouth, and it felt like I was suffocating. As you can imagine this fear lingers on – even though my current dentist is great and I realise that most dentists won't allow their patients to choke to death! One way to help your Fearful Child deal with its fears is to remind it that you do actually now have all the inner resources you need to deal with most situations you will encounter. To help your Fearful Child find the resources to deal with a particular situation, use the 'Seven steps to anchoring resourcefulness' exercise, along with positive anchors and triggers (both in Part 4).

Transform your beliefs
Your Fearful Child's fears will be driven by your beliefs. These might be beliefs about yourself, a situation or the other people involved. Our Fearful Child often has sets of beliefs that are not going to help us in dealing with the variety of situations that we face. Use the 'Transforming you beliefs' exercise at the end of Part 4 to help you to create more supportive and empowering beliefs.

What does your Fearful Child need?
Just think about a child in front of you who is scared. What they need is reassurance, love, hand-holding, patience, advice and support to develop the confidence and the ability to deal with different situations that they fear. What they don't need is ridicule, anger and frustration, which is often what our inner critic throws at our own Fearful Child.

My five-year-old nephew is full of confidence in most circumstances, but entering the dungeons of Warwick Castle he made sure that my arms were tightly wrapped around him as he stood in front of me. This sort of reassurance is just the kind of thing that our Fearful Child needs, no matter how old we are.

I promise I won't close the door when you get frightened...

Think of a situation where your Fearful Child might get scared.
What do you need to do in this situation that will make you
feel confident and relaxed?
What can you do to care for your Fearful Child to ensure that
you achieve this?

Be your own best friend

One thing I have realised about the inner critic is that we often say
things to ourselves that we would not dare to say to our best friends –
in fact we probably would not even think those things of our friends.
Yet here we are berating and belittling ourselves. Many people are not
their own best friend; in fact, they are often their own worst enemy.
This can have a variety of effects on them. It can:

- Decrease their confidence.
- Demotivate and demoralise them.
- Stop them from realising their dreams and using their talents.
- Stop them from enjoying what they do and
  their achievements.
- Make them overwork, leading to ill health and stress.
- Make them fail to ask for support.

When your inner critic kicks in it is worth saying to yourself:

Q. Would you say that to your best friend?
Q. What would your best friend say to you right now?
Q. What would you say to a friend who was in your situation?

*'The hardest person to get to know is yourself. Get to know yourself
and have a friend for life.'*

Peter Karsten

Part 6

Your Inner Critic and Other People

You might be wondering why there is a Part dealing with other people in a book about your inner critic. There are two reasons for this. Firstly, our inner critic and our Fearful Child can make it difficult for us to handle criticism from others. Secondly, our inner critic can influence our view of others around us and we can become critical of them.

This Part will assist you in dealing with the comments passed by others, as well as learning to appreciate and even praise and forgive others, who might be different from you. As you learn to master your inner critic you can develop more constructive relationships with others that are not fuelled by your perfectionism or your inner critic.

How to handle criticism from others

What is the difference between criticism and feedback?

When I am working in organisations people often use the term 'constructive criticism'. However, by its very nature, criticism is never going to be as constructive as feedback. Criticism is about passing a judgement about what is right and wrong; it is usually about finding fault with another person, perhaps fuelled by the giver's own inner critic. Therefore a lot of criticism hurts, wounds and can undermine our confidence. Feedback, on the other hand, provides information about things that have gone well or that could be changed. It provides helpful advice on how we have done and how we might improve.

The problem with criticism from others is that it can either feed into our fears or our inner critic, sparking an emotional reaction in us and not helping us to deal with them in an entirely adult way.

There are three aspects of handling any criticism from others:

- Understanding where the comments are coming from.
- Managing your reaction to criticism.
- Finding a way to respond to the comments.

Understanding where the comments are coming from

'If someone criticises you unjustly, it is important to express your disagreement but also invite the other person to clarify what has prompted the criticism.'

Anne Dickson

Once you are able to understand why the person is saying what they are saying it becomes much easier to respond to their comments.

If we think about ourselves for a moment and why we end up criticising others we can recognise that we are often critical at the times when we are feeling unhappy, insecure, under-confident or frustrated. The following three points can help us in understanding what is behind people's comments, whether they are being reasonable and if you need to listen to the feedback.

Step into their shoes

This technique is described in 'Stepping into someone else's shoes' later in this Part and it can be used here to great effect. If you have someone in your life – a parent, family member, manager, colleague or even a friend – who often criticises you, then you might find it useful to step into their shoes and to think about what is driving their behaviour and comments.

When I did this with a friend who would often make small throwaway comments that were less than constructive, I realised that as a working mother she was very stressed and not entirely happy with her life. Her little criticisms were just a sign of this, and not something to be taken personally.

What mood are they in?

Our mood affects how we behave and what we say, so thinking about the mood of the other person can help you to see their comments in a different context. The Mood Map at the start of Part 4 might help you to think about this. Their comments might say more about their mood, rather than what you are doing.

Do they have your best interests at heart?

Sometimes friends, family or even colleagues do have your best interests are heart. What they are saying might be true, it is just that they are not very skilled at putting things across. Or their fears and concerns for you mean that it does not come across in the right way. Thinking about their intention can help to understand what they have said.

Managing your reaction to criticism

In order to respond in a calm, measured way we first need to be able to manage our response to criticism. We will often experience the 'flight or fight' response first of all, which can trigger either our Fearful Child, making us want to run away, or our Critical Parent, making us want to stay and fight. Neither response is going to be helpful. You need to be able to manage the emotional response using some of the ideas and techniques in Part 4, so that you can engage your Adult mode and respond in a calm, logical way. You will then be ready to listen to their point of view objectively and put your perspective over in a rational way.

Finding a way to respond to the comments

'For most of us, put-downs are more effectively handled with honesty and clarity than with an attempt at wit.'

Anne Dickson

If we are either going to respond to what someone is saying to us or discuss their tendency to criticise, then we need to do it in a timely way, in a calm and constructive manner. There is no point in throwing criticisms at others if you want them to stop criticising you.

Reframing what people say to you

Just as you can reframe the messages from your own inner critic (see 'Choose the right frame', Part 3) you can also use the same process to reframe what people say to you. This will then help you when you respond to their less than helpful comments. When you start to do this, you might want to do it in your own mind first of all. Once you have mastered the art of turning criticisms into positives, start to say it out loud to the person concerned. For example:

Criticisms from others…	Your reframed response to them…
'You're hopeless with money.'	'We do have a different approach/philosophy to money' or 'There is certainly a thing or two I could learn about money from how you approach it.'
'You are so moody/you cry too easily.'	'Yes, I am in touch with my emotions.'
'You'll never be able to do X/become Y.'	'Yes, it certainly will be a challenge' or 'Yes, this is a big challenge to rise to.'
'You always look so scruffy.'	'We do have a very different sense of style.'
'You're so clumsy.'	'Like everyone, I am only human.'

Q. What criticisms have been said to you?
Q. How can you reframe them?

Who says so?

Who do you listen to in life? Whose opinion do you value most? Your wise self? Your inner critic? Other people? Do you only listen to other people's opinions and discount your own viewpoint or do you discount what others say? Obviously, a mixture of the two is important to keep things in perspective. With a strong inner critic, what often happens is that we only listen to other people's opinions that back up the inner critic's viewpoint, and discount the positive feedback we get from others or ignore our inner wisdom.

> **Q.** Whose opinion do you value most?
>
> **Q.** Whose opinions help to support you in your life?

In order to lead a happy and successful life it is important to seek out people who will support, nurture, inspire and challenge you in a constructive way.

Whose opinion should you take on board?

Are there some people in your life whose opinions seem to be in cahoots with your inner critic? I ask this question because our inner critic can often lead us to listen to the comments and opinions of others that are destructive and undermine our confidence and happiness. It does not mean that you should discount all negative feedback that you get. I really value those friends and colleagues who give me honest feedback in a supportive and constructive manner, that will help me to develop myself. With others it might be about ignoring or avoiding people when they are not in a constructive mood as what they say and how they say it is likely to tap into your inner critic. Or you might want to check out their comments with those people you value, who are likely to give you a more balanced viewpoint.

Gaining an objective view of feedback

By managing your own reactions to feedback you can step back and take a more objective view of the feedback or criticisms that you receive. I now find that when I look at evaluations following a workshop, I can celebrate all the positive comments and look to learn from any feedback that I get about how I might improve and enhance the programmes that I run.

People who support your dreams

Part of deciding whose opinions you take notice of is about having people in your environment who support your dreams. Whether they are about your career, where you want to live, activities you want to take up, it is important that you have people around you whose comments will encourage and assist you in fulfilling your dreams. This is especially so when our inner critic is still strong and if our Fearful Child is holding us back. You probably want to avoid people who tell you that your dreams are impossible.

Q. Is there a dream that you have that you have not fulfilled because someone said it was impossible?

Q. Are there people you can talk to who are likely to support you in fulfilling your dreams?

'We need to hold fast to our dreams. Don't let the enemy of doubt take them. Our hopes and vision for the future are certainly as valid as any doubt or fear. By holding to them, as in a great storm, we can actualise them.'

Barbara Cahill

Stepping into someone else's shoes

Our inner critic can often stop us from seeing other people's perspective and it can give us the impression that only its viewpoint is valid. This can then fuel our critical attitude towards others. One way to counter this is to step into the shoes of the person that we are struggling to understand.

Seeing things from their perspective

We all step into other people's shoes to some extent, but some people do this more than others; they tend to be more understanding and tolerant of other people. Others ask, 'What would I do if I was in their situation?' – but this is putting *yourself* in their shoes, not stepping into *their* shoes and seeing things from *their* perspective. Ask yourself, 'If I was X what would I be thinking and feeling?'.

There is an exercise that I use myself and with clients when coaching them or on my workshops. It works best if you actually move around while doing the exercise. As you move from your shoes, to the other person's shoes and through the whole exercise, it produces a profound shift in how you think and feel and will impact on your behaviour with the person later on.

How to step into another person's shoes

Think of someone whom you would like to understand better; this could be a colleague, family member or friend.

Step 1: In your own shoes

Stand somewhere private, where you have space to move around. Now imagine the other person standing or sitting opposite you. Take a look at the other person. As you look at them:

What are you thinking?
What are you feeling?
What are you experiencing in your body?

Step 2: In their shoes

Now move to stand in the other person's shoes. Imagine that you are now them, with their job, family, home, hobbies, interests whatever you know about them or can imagine about them. Rest assured you can do this even if you know little about them. Now as them:

What are you thinking?
What are you feeling?
What are you experiencing in your body?

Step 3: Your wise self

Now you need to move out of their shoes and step into a place where you can view the interaction between yourself and the other person. Here you step into your wise self. As your wise self, who can look objectively and wisely at the situation, look back at yourself in Step 1 and ask yourself:

What do you want to say to yourself over there that will help you deal with this situation?
What words of wisdom and guidance can you give you over there about your relationship with this other person?

Step 4: Back in your own shoes (where you were in Step 1)

Move back to where you were in Step 1 and into your own shoes again. Take on board the words of wisdom and then ask yourself what are you now thinking, experiencing and feeling. Notice what has changed in you.

Q. Can you think of anyone whose shoes it would be useful to step into?

How people have used this exercise:

- A workshop participant who specialises in working with challenging and disruptive students used it to step into the shoes of a particular student she was seeing on a one-to-one basis when she was feeling very stuck on how to help the young person move forward.
- A coaching client was finding it a challenge to manage one of her team members.
- Another client was struggling with being a full-time working mum and did this exercise twice, firstly to step into her manager's shoes and then into her daughter's.

Many of my training programmes are ongoing and occasionally there can be an individual who is a challenge, and I might be in danger of either having my Critical Parent or Fearful Child triggered. Many times I have used this exercise to gain a new perspective on the situation and engage my wise self to find new ways of dealing with the interactions and change the relationship into a more constructive one.

———•———

Stop criticising others

There are few of us with inner critics who do not also criticise others. This might not be out loud, to their face or even behind their backs. However, even if it is just in our head it still has a negative effect on our contentment with life and on our relationships.

Stopping criticising others does not mean that if someone is behaving unreasonably or is not respecting our own or others' rights we do not do anything about it. Rather it is the difference between being clear about what is unreasonable behaviour and dealing with it in an assertive manner, versus nit-picking because things are not how you would want them to be. As with our criticisms of ourselves, our criticisms of others are often unreasonable, based on the tyranny of perfection or wanting everyone to be like us, to have our approach to life and our beliefs.

Recovering control freak

I admit that I am a recovering control freak. Our criticisms of others are often about us wanting them to behave in a way that will suit us. We want to be able to control the world around us, even if we do not verbalise our criticisms of others.

Are you a control freak? Think back over the last week how many times have you either thought or said out loud comments that were critical of others or where you have wrapped up criticisms as questions, for example:

'Have you thought about cooking the pasta this way…?'
'Have you tried X route to work, it might be quicker?'
'Wouldn't the blue shirt go better with that tie?'

You might think these are helpful suggestions or questions, but it all depends on what mode they are coming from, Critical Parent or wise mentor, and whether the advice has been asked for in the first place. Even if you don't say these things out loud they will seep out in some way – your tone of voice, your body language – which others will pick up on.

Think back over the last month.
List the criticisms that you have thought or said out loud.
Alongside your list, give each criticism a rating on a scale of 1 (very constructive, helpful) to 10 (very controlling, unnecessary or even destructive).
Be honest with yourself when you rate how helpful your thoughts and comments were.

Learn to drop it!

People are different – otherwise, life would be very boring. But this does mean that sometimes we need to shut up and let some things go. By praising other people and appreciating their differences, the negative comments both in our heads and coming out of our mouths will decrease and may even stop, unless they are truly justified. To help you to do this spot when you were about to say something less than positive or constructive, rate it on a scale of 1 to 10 (1 = very constructive, helpful to 10 = very controlling, unnecessary or even destructive) and decide whether it is really going to help the situation, and your relationship with the individual. Sometimes it is far more constructive to drop it, to ignore what someone has said or done. You might even start to focus on the positive things they say and do.

Think before speaking

We know that comments made by others can hurt us, but we don't always stop to think before we speak. Throwaway comments can often end up hurting others and passing our own negativity onto them. I was speaking to someone recently who had been hurt by a negative comment made by someone when she was showing her grandson's wedding photos. The throwaway comment had really hurt her, but like many people she had not said so at the time. However, the impact of this negative comment lives on today and into the future.

Have there been moments recently when you have made a throwaway comment that might have hurt or angered another? Was the comment really necessary? Rather than beat yourself up about it and get into a vicious circle, practise valuing people's differences and even praising others to create a virtuous circle.

A simple apology

None of us are perfect and there are times when we might be in a less than resourceful state and may say things that have intentionally, or unintentionally, hurt someone else. When this happens I go back and apologise for what I said or did. Interestingly, some people can be unaware of the so-called slight or harsh word, or, if they were aware of it, the apology is always a welcome surprise. Rather than turn the situation into a guilt trip, with severe beatings from your inner critic, a simple apology can be enough to rectify things and move on.

But what about people who really annoy us?

Most of us have one or two (OK, even more than that) annoying habits or behaviours. If you are on the receiving end of annoying behaviour, and it is not hurting you, then think before you criticise, pass comment or attempt to change the person. Is it just about your need for perfection, to be right in everything (even how a report is written, the washing up is done or beds are made)? Can you learn to live with or even love the habit or behaviour? Have you thought how annoying your perfectionism and control freakery is?

The following techniques will help you to appreciate other people and their so-called 'annoying habits':

See things from their perspective

One way to help you see the other person in a different light is by stepping into their shoes and seeing things from their perspective. The exercise in the previous section will enable you to do this and it will provide you with new insights into why a particular person behaves in the way they do. For example, I had a manager on an ongoing programme whose behaviour and attitude easily hooked my Critical Parent. In fact most people reacted to him in this way, and although he had worked in the organisation for many years he had few allies. I decided that I needed to change my attitude and approach to him and I did the stepping into his shoes exercise. When I stepped into his shoes I gained a sense of how lonely it must be to work everyday with people who don't particularly like you. I was then able to develop a much more compassionate attitude and approach towards him that meant I was able to work with him in an adult-to-adult way, rather than ending up in Critical Parent mode.

See the person and not the behaviour

Before I did a lot of personal and professional development, and when I still had a very strong inner critic, I would be quick to judge other people. Peter, a colleague and friend of mine, would encourage me to see the person behind the behaviour, which at the time I found very difficult to do. However, having learnt to master my inner critic and become more patient and understanding of others, I am now able to do this in most situations.

You might be wondering how you go about 'seeing the person behind the behaviour'. There are a number of things you can do to assist you in this process:

- Step into their shoes and recognise that their behaviour might be saying more about the mood they are in than anything else.
- Recognise that what might be driving their behaviour is their own Fearful Child or inner critic, so taking a more compassionate approach can be more beneficial than just reacting to their behaviour.
- Control your reactions, watch out that your Fearful, Rebellious or Sulky Child is not triggered, or your Critical, Controlling Parent
- Respond from your wise self and your Adult mode and in time you will be able to bring this out in the other person and have an adult-to-adult conversation.

By doing this I find that instead of getting hooked by other people's negative behaviour and even thinking less of them because of it, I now can see the person behind the behaviour and communicate with that part of them. Usually this approach of respecting them as a person quickly turns the situation around.

What if you need to give someone some feedback?

Obviously it is not good to keep quiet while someone walks all over us. If someone's behaviour or comments have hurt us then managing our reactions and responding in a calm and adult way is appropriate.

Mastering your inner critic will help you to be far more tolerant of others. It will allow you to see past their behaviour and see them as human beings with foibles, hang-ups, strengths and weaknesses.

There is a balance between rushing in and saying something too soon when you are still angry or hurt, and stewing so long over something that it becomes even bigger than it was, and comes out in the wrong way. Leaving things for too long and tackling them in the wrong way can create as much havoc as the original slight made against you, further harming your relationship. Part 4 on Managing Your Mood contains lots of ideas to assist you in staying calm, which will help you to respond to people in an assertive manner.

Q. Are there people that you need to talk to about something?

Q. Are there some situations where leaving it too long has made it worse for you?

Start praising others

Praising others can act as a counterbalance to criticising others and will have a positive impact on you and your life. It will help you to be a more positive person; you will create more positive feelings around you and what you give out will come back to you.

In praise of others
There are different ways of praising others...

Praise on the inside
Praising others can be something that you just do internally. It is about seeing the positive side of people and what they say and do. If you find yourself about to criticise someone in your head, stop, step into their shoes and find something positive about them. Determine each day to see the positive side of people you meet, situations you are in, and places you go to. Understanding other people's lives and the moods they are in can help you to be more sympathetic towards them.

Celebrate the differences
Now that I am more confident about who I am, I am better able to value the differences in other people around me. I am able to acknowledge, celebrate and respect the different things that people bring to the party, whether this is colleagues, family members or friends. If someone does start to irritate me it is usually because of our differences and stepping back and celebrating those helps me to gain a better perspective on the situation.

Praise out loud
People are often not used to being praised and do not necessarily know how to react to it. I was staying in a hotel running two workshops with quite challenging groups of managers. One of the treats of that particular trip was the amazing vegetarian food in the hotel. Each meal had imaginative and well-executed dishes – it was a real pleasure eating there. So on the last evening I asked to see the head chef, who came out of the kitchen looking like a startled

rabbit about to be shot. I think he was so shocked to get praise I am not sure he even took it on board. Even though people might not know how to react to praise, still do it. They will in time be able to take it on board and perhaps if more of us complimented others, we would get used to it and be able to bask in the glory of it.

Q. Who do you now value for their differences?
Q. What do they bring to your life?

Inner critic view of praise

The inner critic by its very nature is not given to praising ourselves or others. And because it often aims at 100 per cent perfection it does not think people are worthy of praise if something does not come up to scratch. But as seen in the section on 'The tyranny of perfection' you rarely meet a happy perfectionist! So ignore the little voice that says about your friends, family members and colleagues, 'Yes but they didn't do X' or 'They still do Y that is annoying' – just go ahead and praise them. Thank them for the things they do, tell them what you value and appreciate them for.

Who could you praise more of the time?

Praise and celebrate friends, family members, colleagues, neighbours and even complete strangers (I often get complimented by complete strangers on a particular pair of earrings that my brother bought me and I'm always happy to receive these compliments).

Q. Who could you silently or directly praise?
Q. What are you praising them for?

People's reaction to praise

Many of us are not very good at taking on board praise, whether it is about our achievements, our clothes, the presentation we have done or the meal we have created. People say things like:

'What, this old thing?'
'It was nothing.'
'I still have not done X and Y.'
'Such and such did better than me.'

But just because people brush praise aside does not mean that we should stop giving it. It has taken me a long time to just say 'thank you' when someone praises me, with no denial, no explanation, just thanks. If you find other people are uncomfortable in the face of praise, keep on going, they will get more used to it and start to enjoy it.

You could also try sending someone a card. If you put your praise or thanks in writing, they can't shrug it off quite so easily, and they will have lasting proof to counter their own inner critic.

Forgiving others

Those of us with a strong inner critic often find it hard to forgive ourselves, let alone other people. We have such high standards that they are impossible to meet and therefore others can continually fall short and commit some act of disappointment or hurt, which is hard to forgive.

Forgive yourself first

Once you have accepted that you are only human, and therefore susceptible to making mistakes, it is easier to start to accept this in others. This is the way to freedom and happiness. As SARK says in her book *Living Juicy*:

'I forgive myself
I forgive everyone
I am totally free'

I love the idea that forgiveness leads to total freedom. We are free from either the guilt inside us or resentment and bitterness towards others.

How do you go about forgiving others?

If we hang onto past hurts and end up blaming others for how we feel, then we are carrying around a heavy load and it is going to be difficult to move on to be totally happy and at peace with the world.

Forgiving others can involve a number of different processes and of course does depend on the level of hurt caused. If the act was extreme a counsellor or coach might be needed to help you in the process of forgiveness.

However, what I am focussing on here is the so-called slights and mistakes people make that, because of our strong inner critics, we might find hard to let go of. Many of the processes already mentioned will assist you with moving on:

- **Separate out the behaviour from the person**
  – remember the person behind the behaviour, maybe remember all their great qualities or things that they have done in the past.
- **Step into their shoes** – there might be a very good reason why they have not returned your answerphone message or written a thank-you card, or why they ignored you in the corridor at work.
- **Learn to deal with your own hurt** – you might need to deal with your own negative feelings in order to enable you to move on. The exercises in Part 4 on Managing Your Mood will assist you in this process.

- **Tap into your wise self** – what words of wisdom can you give yourself to assist you in the process of forgiving?

Q. Who have you already forgiven?
Q. Who do you need to forgive, in order to move on?

'In terms of personal happiness, you cannot be peaceful while at the same time blaming others.'

Richard Carlson

Part 7

Moving to Action

'Success is 99 per cent failure.'

Soichiro Honda

Sometimes change happens quickly, almost immediately, while other changes might take longer to bring about. Mastering your inner critic, which probably has been with you for years, if not your whole lifetime, often needs ongoing concerted effort.

This Part provides you with support and ideas to assist you in keeping going while you are in the process of mastering your inner critic. What you will find is that as you use these techniques on a regular basis you will create a momentum, until you reach a 'tipping point' when suddenly change becomes rapid and almost automatic. Remember that relapses or slipping back into old ways are merely there to help you to learn more, rather than being something to beat yourself up about.

Where do you start to change?

I remember having a conversation with a colleague of mine and an NLP master practitioner before I trained in NLP. We were talking about change, especially personal change, and I was saying that it can be so hard to bring about, often involving a real struggle with lots of resistance, and that it can take a long time. The NLP practitioner said, 'No, change is easy and simple.' I stood there thinking, 'No it isn't,' but was intrigued and wanted to find out more, which eventually led me to train as an NLP master practitioner. The following is based on world-renowned NLP practitioner Robert Dilts' Logical Levels of Change model.

Levels of change

When something has been part of you for a long time it can be hard to think of where to start to make changes. If change seems hard or if it takes a long time, it can be because we are approaching the change in the wrong way. The following model can help you to identify where you need to start the change process to make it much easier and quicker.

For change to be quick and easy we need to identify at which level or levels we need to make the change. For example, if you want to be more assertive, you can learn various assertive behaviours. However, if you have a belief that runs counter to this behaviour, the belief is likely to hinder you. So if you believe 'I'm not an assertive person', 'If I say no I will upset people or they won't like me' or 'If I speak up I may lose my job' it is unlikely that you will feel confident and be assertive.

You can use the model below to identify where your block is and where you need to make changes:

Spirit	What else?
Identity	Who?
Beliefs	Why?
Competence	How?
Behaviour	What?
Environment	Where/when?

What does each level mean?

You can apply this model to any aspect of your life, but here we are going to apply it to the topic of supporting yourself to see how each level relates to this topic. The reason for exploring this is that often our inner critic can cause us to not look after and support ourselves.

We are going to start at the level of environment and work our way up to the level of spirit. However, we can go in at any level to bring about change. The trick is to identify the right level to make the changes for your own personal situation. It often appears easier to make changes at the lower levels, but actually the more profound changes frequently happen when we work at the level of beliefs and identity. Once you have made changes at the higher levels usually everything else falls into place.

Environment

This is about *where* and *when* things happen. In terms of support it might be about making sure that you have:

- A home and work environment (and relationships) which will support you.
- Time for activities that will support you physically, emotionally and socially.
- People in your life who are positive, supportive and appreciative.

- Books, quotes, pictures, etc. that you can turn to for inspiration.

Behaviour

This is about *what* you do – are your behaviours positive and supportive? For example: eating healthily, getting enough sleep, taking exercise, writing in a journal to help you to process issues, or appreciating what you do by writing in your Brag Bag.

Competence

In this model competence refers to *how* you represent things inside your head – the pictures and messages that are going on in your mind. These pictures and messages have a profound impact on your feelings and behaviour. For example, making sure that the pictures or the messages in your head are positive and supportive will help you to feel good about yourself, motivated, enthusiastic and happy. See the exercise on page 121 in Part 4 that shows the powerful link between the thoughts and pictures in your head and how you feel.

Beliefs

This is about *why* we do things – our beliefs about the situation we are in and the world as a whole impact on how we view events, how we react to them and our behaviour. For example, if you believe that 'Asking for support is a sign of weakness' or that 'My partner, boss or children will never change and be helpful', these beliefs can easily become self-fulfilling prophecies and stop you from taking actions to support yourself.

We tend to go through life without necessarily being aware of the range of beliefs that we have and the profound effect that they have on how we react to others, to events, and the impact that this has on our feelings and behaviour. The 'Transforming your beliefs' exercise at the end of Part 4 explores ways of changing your beliefs to help you ensure that your beliefs are positive, supportive and empowering.

Identity

This concerns *who* you are and beliefs about yourself, which in turn affect how you feel and drive your behaviour. For example, having the belief 'I am a strong person, I don't need any help' or 'I am a highly-strung person' will have a strong hold on your behaviour.

We often walk around and live our lives with beliefs about ourselves that are no longer relevant and perhaps never were. Most of these beliefs will be negative and can easily be used as ammunition by your inner critic.

Spirit

This is about *what* or *who else* there is in life. It is about the bigger picture and our connections with everything around us. It is our 'spiritual' self or life in the widest context.

I like to view this as being about whatever raises your mood, enables you to see the bigger picture and makes you feel positive about life. The spiritual level can be different things for different people. For some, nature lifts their spirits, for others, it is music, time on their own, dancing, meditating, laughing with friends.

Many people live very hectic lives, commuting, working long hours, caring for children or elderly parents, getting fit, letting their hair down, with little thought about 'what or who else' is in their lives and they sometimes stop and wonder what is the point to it all. Being able to see the bigger picture, keeping things in perspective, can help us deal with the challenges that life throws at us.

Logical levels at work – supporting and caring for yourself

Think about the topic of supporting and caring for yourself, then answer the following questions:

What helps you in supporting and caring for yourself? (e.g. being around supportive people, writing in a journal, having some time to yourself)

What hinders you in supporting and caring for yourself? (e.g. not having any personal space to be on your own; getting sucked into caring for others, while forgetting your own needs; thinking you don't have time to take care of yourself)

At what level or levels is this block? (e.g. level of environment for 'not having any personal space to be on your own'; level of beliefs for 'thinking you don't have time to take care of yourself')

What action can you take to make changes at this level, to overcome this block or minimise the impact that it has on you? (e.g. transform beliefs to assist you in taking some time for yourself)

Using the logical levels in your life

Think of something you want to change in your life, for example:

- Learning to say no without feeling guilty.
- Asking for more support at work.
- Wanting to feel confident when presenting ideas in a meeting.
- Mastering your inner critic.
- Learning a new language.

Now ask yourself the following questions…

Environment

When is the best time to tackle this situation or make this change? Where is the best place to do this?

Behaviour
What behaviours will help you in this situation?

Competence
When you think of this situation, what pictures do you see in your head or mind's eye? What messages/thoughts can you hear in your head?

Beliefs/Identify
What beliefs do you have regarding the following:
This situation?
Yourself in this situation?
The other person or people in this situation?
Are these beliefs going to help or hinder you? If they are not going to help you, what might be a more helpful belief(s) to have?

Spirit/Purpose
What keeps you going, what helps you to get things in perspective? What lifts your spirit, motivates you to keep going in these kinds of situations?

> **Q.** What other issues are you facing in your life that you could apply the Logical Levels of Change to?

Changing habits of a lifetime

I often hear clients, family and friends saying things like 'You can't teach an old dog new tricks' or 'A leopard can't change its spots'. I'm no dog trainer so I can't comment on dogs and I know that leopards probably keep their spots for life, but I do know about people. From what I see and hear it does seem that us human beings are infinitely adaptable and capable of change if we want to change. After all, there's the huge amount of 'silver surfers' on the Internet (including my dad who knows more about it than me); many 60, 70, 80-year-olds taking up new hobbies (my aunt and mum took up watercolour painting in their sixties), people in their eighties who are leaping out of aeroplanes on charity sky-diving jumps. So it seems if you really want to change or learn something new, age is not a barrier.

Habits form our life

Most of us have habitual ways of doing things from when we get up in the morning to when we go to bed at night. Most of these habits are routine and harmless and some will be positive. Others, like losing our temper at the slightest irritation or comfort eating when we feel low, might not be that helpful if we want to lead a healthy and happy life.

Listening to our inner critic is just another habit that we have in our lives. We get used to its tirades and even used to how bad it makes us feel. At certain times, during certain phases of your day, week or year you might let your thoughts go wild with the old criticisms. However, when we put our minds to it, we can change the habits associated with our inner critic and thereby learn to master it.

Your own positive and negative habits

Positive thinking patterns I get into:	Negative thinking patterns I get into:
Positive habits that support me in being healthy and happy:	Negative habits that hinder me in being healthy and happy:

Creating new positive habits – repetition creates habits

It is said that you need to do something between 15 and 20 times before it becomes a habit. So if you have a wastepaper bin in your office or kitchen and you move it, it will take about 15 to 20 goes at throwing your rubbish where the bin used to be before you remember where it now is. Most of the things that we want to change in our lives are a bit more complicated than moving the position of your waste bin, so they will require more thought and effort. You might want to set up some reminders, supports and rewards to help you in changing how you think, feel and behave in order to master your inner critic.

Understanding a little about the process of change and how we learn to do new things can help us to take control of the process and to support ourselves during the times of change.

Becoming unconsciously competent

The model below is used to describe the process that you go through when you are starting to learn something, whether this is learning a new language, to master your inner critic, to drive or to juggle. Think about something you are changing in yourself or learning to do. Then use the model below to think about which stage you are at. I have used the example of writing down your appreciations.

Unconscious incompetence

Before you start to learn something you don't know how much you don't know! Ignorance is bliss.

In terms of writing down appreciations, before you start you might not even be aware that there is anything to appreciate yourself for as you might be so used to listening to your inner critic berating you for so many years.

Conscious incompetence

This is where learning can be painful, as you become very aware of what you don't know and your weaknesses. People can often give up at this stage.

When you first go to write your appreciations you might find it very difficult if not impossible to do. You might even feel tearful at the idea that you have nothing to appreciate yourself for or that in the past you have been so nasty and critical of yourself.

Conscious competence

This stage can feel awkward. You are starting to do the new behaviour, but you are very aware of everything you do. You can feel like you are not yourself, and the new behaviour is not you. People say that they feel like they are 'acting'. Again people often give up at this stage – but it is only with repetition that the new skill or behaviour becomes part of you.

Writing down your appreciations in your Brag Bag may feel really odd and even difficult at first. You might think that you are forcing yourself to write them, not really believing them at first. However with practice it will become natural to you.

Unconscious competence

This is where the new skills, behaviour, etc. become second nature or habitual; where you end up behaving or doing the new thing without thinking about it.

Once you have become experienced at writing down appreciations you will start to be naturally appreciative of your own (and others') strengths. In the end it becomes something you do unconsciously, perhaps without the need to even write them down.

Slipping from unconscious competence to unconscious incompetence

It is possible that, without conscious effort to reflect on what we are doing, we end up going from unconscious competence back to unconscious incompetence. We can get sloppy in how we do things. Think about most people's driving ability some years after they pass their test – they fall into many pitfalls that would lead them to fail a test if they took it again today. We need to stay alert to ensure that the old inner critic does not slip back in when our guard is down.

Remind yourself to change

When we are attempting to retrain how we think and master our inner critic it is useful to use some reminders to act as prompts as we go about our daily lives. These could be:

- Post-its around your house, by your computer, on your fridge.
- A postcard on your notice board that reminds you to be positive, manage your mood, appreciate yourself – nobody else needs to know why it is there.
- Reminders in your diary.
- Writing a postcard to yourself and getting a friend to post it to you in a few weeks' time.

Try to identify where you are most likely to need these reminders. For example, I realised that it is often when I am on the phone or computer that I say yes to some new request for my time or even volunteer to take on even more things. So I have put sticky smiley faces on both my phones and my computer so that I am reminded to stop and think before accepting or volunteering.

Q. What reminders are you going to use?

A practical experiment – to act as a reminder

If you are wearing a watch then take it off your usual hand and put it onto the other one (usually quite a feat in itself, involving awkward manoeuvring). Firstly, take a look at your watch on your different hand: how does it look and feel? People on workshops where I have done this have said things like:

'I don't like my watch any more!'
'It does not look like my hand/arm!'
'It feels awkward/tight/wrong.'

This is equivalent to the conscious incompetence stage, as you have not got used to wearing it on the other hand.

Now wear it this way for at least 20 days. If you take it off at night, in the morning you might first go to put it on your usual hand and then remember. As you go through the day you will start off looking at your blank wrist, until it becomes a new habit to look at the other one. Let this be a reminder and metaphor for the other changes that you want to make in your life.

If you don't wear a watch, perhaps wear one for the next 20 days as a reminder of other things you want to change.

Another little exercise we do on courses when discussing change is to ask everyone to fold their arms in the normal way, then fold them the other way around. You might like to try this as well.

It probably took you a short while to figure out how to do this, maybe with a bit of flapping of hands and arms. Once you have got it, you might be sat there feeling a bit awkward, certainly not as comfortable as you were when you folded them in your usual way.

Such simple, unconscious behaviour is habitual, so doing it another way feels difficult and awkward. This might also be the case when you are changing something more fundamental about yourself. However, with practice and time it will come naturally to you. Just because something feels awkward, it doesn't mean it is wrong for you.

On the road to mastering my inner critic I found that, once things had begun to change for the better, there were times when I felt free of worry and quite happy. But as this was so unfamiliar to me I would start to worry! I would think: 'Maybe I am being too complacent, it will all come crashing down around me.' Gradually, as my new ways of thinking, feeling and behaving became more habitual, I felt comfortable with the new feeling of calmness and confidence, rather than strange and awkward.

Slipping back into old ways

In his book *Slimming With Pete*, Pete Cohen talks about lapsing, relapsing and collapsing. The great thing is that even with a complete collapse you can learn from it and start over again in a much more powerful way as you have learned from your experience. As Dr Wayne W. Dyer says in his wonderful little book *Staying on the Path*:

'If you slip it does not mean you are less valuable. It simply means you have something to learn from slipping.'

Here are some examples of lapses that people often experience along the journey to mastering their inner critic:

- They forget to listen to their whole self (Fearful Child, Fun Child, Nurturing Parent, etc.) until they find themselves at a dead end. However, by identifying what gets in the way of them taking time to do this they can create a plan of how to do it in the future.
- They allow other people's comments to get to them, which in turn triggers their inner critic or Fearful Child.
- Life is so busy and/or challenging that the Fun Child does not get a look in.

- A mistake is made and they let their inner critic beat them up relentlessly.
- They forget to care for the Fearful Child and this holds them back from making decisions or fulfilling dreams.

What usually happens when you slip up?

Do you end up criticising yourself, beating yourself up, feeling bad, feeling guilt and/or giving up?

None of this will help or motivate you to move on. In fact, constantly berating yourself is more likely to keep you stuck in your relapsed or collapsed position.

Think about what triggered your relapse.
Were you under a lot of pressure and stress?
What mood were you in?
What can you do differently next time?
Think of times when you have relapsed.
What triggered this?
What can you do differently next time?
What is your first step in moving forward from here?

From this day forth...

There is a Buddhist term called 'honi-myo' which means being able to make a fresh cause in each new moment or starting each day afresh. Whatever happened yesterday or an hour ago – good or bad – it is now that counts: today is the start of the rest of your life. You can start over each moment, each day, creating more positive causes for your health and happiness.

The great thing about this is that you are always starting over. You can kick your inner critic to one side and get on with the business at hand rather than worrying about what happened yesterday. Learn from it and move on.

―•―

Don't 'try', just do it!

'Life is either a daring adventure or nothing.'

Helen Keller

'Don't 'try', just do it!' might seem like a comment from the inner critic, but it is something I often talk about on my workshops and there is something about that little word 'try' that can trip us up.

You know what it is like if you say to someone:

'I'll try and make it to your party.'
'I'll try and get the report done by the deadline.'
'I'll try and exercise more in the New Year.'
'I'll try to be more assertive.'

There is almost an unspoken 'but… I am very busy, I don't hold out much hope that it will work or that I will stick with it.'

When clients say 'I'm going to try…' I always encourage them to 'Just do it.' And there is a big difference in our intention, our determination, when we say 'I am going to lose weight,' 'I am going to be assertive with my boss' and 'I am going to ask for a pay increase.' Saying to yourself or out loud to others what you *are* going to do, rather than what you are going to *try* to do, is much more positive and powerful. When we use 'try' there is always an element of doubt, a lack of conviction.

If you really truly want to do something, then say you'll do it and you will stand a much better chance of doing it. The reason for this is that along with our words come pictures in our head; unconsciously our bodies act out what we are thinking, our thoughts affect how we feel and ultimately our behaviour (see Part 4 on 'Visualising success' for more about the power of visualisation).

Turning 'try' into solid determinations

Since talking about this over the last few years, I still spot myself either saying or about to say the old 'T' word and then rewording it for myself. It is about checking out how strong your determination is, how committed you are to taking action and to changing.

Q. What is it you want to change?

Q. On a scale of 1 (very strong) to 10 (very weak), how strong is your determination?

Q. What can you do to increase your determination?

Ways you can increase your determination

- List all the benefits of changing or taking the action – this can help to convince your conscious and unconscious mind that it is worth doing.
- Visualise how it will be when you are either doing the activity or have reached your goal. See, feel and hear how great it will be. Spend time each day visualising this.
- Check to see if you have any doubts about your ability to succeed. Any doubts will be based on your beliefs: you can use the 'Transforming your beliefs' exercise at the end of Part 4 to assist you in creating beliefs that will support your determination to succeed.

- If your determination or confidence wavers then bring on your cheerleaders, write some appreciations in your Brag Bag to boost your spirits.
- Use the 'Walking into the future' exercise later in this Part to gain further inspiration and increase your determination.

It is OK to decide not to do something

So often we feel that because we have said we are going to do X, we have to follow through or at least be seen to do so.

Our inner critic can so often harass us into thinking that we 'should' do something, and even believing that it is what we want. Hopefully this book has assisted you in sorting out what you really want for yourself and your life, and recognising that there might be some things that have been on your agenda that you now might want to let go of. Sometimes it is because we are not prepared to put the time and effort into something – which is fine. It is better to decide to drop an idea, rather than keep on holding onto it and giving your inner critic something to nag you about!

Positive by-products – positive intentions

There is a theory that all our behaviour provides us with positive by-products or has a positive intention, even our so-called destructive behaviour. We've already talked about the 'tyranny of perfection' and the anxiety, stress and lack of satisfaction it can create. So why do we continue to seek perfection? It's because we do get some positive by-products from this behaviour, whether that's because we succeed in what we do or because it makes us feel in control.

It might be strange to imagine that something that appears to harm us can actually have a positive by-product. But when you think about it, why would we continue to do something that was harmful to us if we were not getting some positive by-product from it?

Positive by-products of your inner critic

These positive by-products might be conscious or unconscious, and only you will know what is true for you. For example, what might be the positive by-products of your inner critic?

- Your inner critic holds you back from doing what you want to do as it says you will be a failure. You therefore don't pursue your dreams, but it also protects you from experiencing the failure that may or may not have occurred had you moved towards your dreams.
- Your inner critic nags you about saying the wrong things and it drives you mad. But it makes you think before you speak and so you don't go and put your foot in it.
- Your constant volunteering and inability to say no might lead you to be overworked and overwhelmed, but it makes you feel needed and valuable as a person.
- Your inner critic makes you highly critical of others, which means that you never get past the first date – but at least you avoid the challenges that a relationship brings up.

Maintaining the positive by-products

If we do not take account of the positive by-products of our negative behaviour, it can be hard to change. Our unconscious mind can sabotage our attempts to change, as it is concerned that it might miss out on these positive by-products. However, it is possible to keep the positive by-products while making sure that the negative behaviour with its destructive consequences is avoided. For example:

Positive by-product of perfectionism:	Positive actions to maintain positive by-product:
You are successful in your work/career because you over-prepare and push yourself. However, this causes you a lot of unnecessary stress and anxiety.	Use positive supports, realistically evaluate your progress, use your cheerleaders, be your own best friend. You can then continue to be successful without the stress and anxiety.
Positive by-product of not pursuing your dreams in case you fail:	**Positive actions to maintain positive by-product:**
You don't have to deal with the failure, the public humiliation, etc.	Realise that setbacks are something to learn from; do not see them as failures, but as stepping stones to success. You take action to ensure that you are successful or to minimise the chances of failure.

It is important that the positive by-products are achieved through taking positive, constructive action rather than continuing with the negative action that is creating other problems.

Your own positive by-products

Q. What are the positive by-products of your inner critic?

Q. What positive actions can you take to maintain these positive by-products, while getting rid of the negative aspects of the inner critic?

Positive intention of your inner critic

A slightly different way of looking at this is that your inner critic has a positive intention in its berating of you. It might not know how to say things with any eloquence, wisdom or compassion, but it might just have something useful to say and have your best interests at heart.

This might be hard to believe, but here are some of the positive things that your inner critic might be wanting for you:

* Wanting you to succeed in life, at work.
* Wanting you to fit in.
* Wanting you to say the right thing and be liked or respected.
* Wanting you to look right and get the right partner.

Q. What does your inner critic say?
Q. What could be the positive intention of this?

Starting to listen to all parts of yourself will help you to engage with your inner critic to uncover its positive intentions (see Part 3 for more about listening to your inner critic and the other parts of yourself).

Inner critic log

It can be useful to create a log of your progress while you are in the process of transforming your inner critic, as the 'glass-is-half-empty' approach to life, perfectionism and dodgy logic can all stop you from seeing the changes that you are making by focussing on what is still wrong. Without a log it is easy for our perfectionist inner critic to tell us we are not progressing, or for our dodgy logic to get in the way of us learning from the experiences that we have. Anything that you use to make your learning more conscious is going to help you to develop yourself and master your inner critic.

Either in your journal or on paper, simply use the following questions to assist you in monitoring your progress and learning from your experiences. It is useful to date your journal so you can see how often your inner critic strikes, as well as recording those times when you successfully mastered your inner critic.

Q. When did the inner critic strike?
Q. What triggered this?
Q. What did it say?
Q. What impact did it have on how you thought, felt and behaved?
Q. What techniques did/can you use to prevent this in the future?

Or:

Q. When were you successful in mastering your inner critic?
Q. What was the situation?
Q. What techniques did you use?
Q. What was the impact on how you thought, felt and behaved?

Turning ideas into action

My aim in writing this book is to help you to transform your inner critic and how you think and feel about yourself. Even if you take only one or two of the ideas from this book and include them in your daily habits, you will notice a difference in your confidence, happiness and motivation. However, to do this you need to turn your ideas into action.

For those of you who like to plan out your actions, the exercise below might be of help. Those of you who prefer a more spontaneous approach might find the visualisation process described in Part 4 useful to think through what you want to do differently.

Clarifying your goals

You might find the following questions beneficial in helping you to clarify your goals and plan out how to achieve them. It's really useful to write your answers down, so that you can refer back to them and check your progress. You might also like to note the date and then set yourself a review date in the future.

Q. What ideas do you want to put into practice?

Q. What benefits will you gain from doing this?

Q. What will you and your life sound, feel and look like when you have done this?

Q. What might stop you from achieving this?

Q. What can you do to overcome this, find a way around it or minimise the impact on you?

Q. Who can you use to support you in taking this action?

Q. How are you going to reward yourself for taking the action?

Keep moving forward

'If you are in hell keep moving forward.'

Mahatma Gandhi

Ever since I heard this quote it has inspired me in all kinds of situations:

- When I was struggling to complete a 69-mile charity bike ride from London to Oxford and was three-quarters of the way through crawling and pushing my bike up over the Chiltern Hills.
- When things don't seem to be changing for the better and I get despondent.
- When I'm feeling at odds with myself on a day off, not knowing what to do with myself. I now know that as long as I do something, never mind what it is, it will move me forward and I will feel better.
- When I've been in the office most of the week and feel rather sluggish. I decide to go out and write my book in a cafe, never mind what I end up writing. Just getting out doing something will make me feel better and move me forward.

Can you think of a time when you felt like you were 'in hell', but kept on moving forward until you eventually came through it?

For some people it is when:

- Their children were first born – the endless sleepless nights...
- Work deadlines loom or there are targets to be met and they think they'll never make it.

- They are suffering from an illness and they feel it will never come to an end.
- They are learning to drive or a new sport and it seems like they will never master it.

Light at the end of the tunnel

There is always a light at the end of the tunnel – it just sometimes seems a long way off or there is a curve in the tunnel and we can't see it, and it feels like we are never getting there. This can happen to all of us. There have been days when all I've wanted to do was crawl under a stone and not face everything I have to do. However, I have learnt how to create some time for self caring and nurturing, in order to help me to keep going. Moving forward little by little.

'Light is just around the corner. You've just got to step out of the dark to see it.'

Peter Karsten

Do you give in or keep going?

The negativity in our life can be very strong and it can seem easier to give in to it rather than fight it. However, from experience I realise that giving in to my negativity will make me feel much worse. On the other hand, if I keep going, take some action to move forward, later I can rest and switch off, while feeling good about what I have done, especially in the face of such negativity. This isn't about denying your feelings: part of moving on might be about doing something positive to release any negative feelings rather than just giving in and being swamped by them.

For example, I sometimes experience this at the end of the working day when I am due to do my evening Buddhist practice. Negativity can slip in, especially if I am tired or feeling down. In the past I might have given in to it, but now I know that if I chant, even for a short while, and determine to change my

mood, I will have a much better evening as a result. You might have noticed this happening when you want to exercise, need to make a tricky phone call or carry out a task which you are not particularly looking forward to. Getting on and doing it will make you feel better than giving in to the negativity.

Q. What can you do to keep on going and come out at the other end?

Q. What can you do to nurture and support yourself in the meantime?

'You will pass through storms, and you may suffer defeat. The essence of the creative life, however, is to persevere in the face of defeat and to follow the rainbow within your heart.'

Daisaku Ikeda

Walking into the future

'Faith is belief in the unseen, the quietly held conviction that even though you can't imagine how, at some time, in some place, in the right way, the thing you desire will indeed come to pass.'

Daphne Rose Kingma

Along with visualising the future, another powerful process that I use both with myself and with clients is walking into the future. This is where you walk along an imaginary line into the future to either explore different futures or work out how you can move towards your dream.

In terms of the inner critic, walking into the future can have a number of benefits. You can move away from its current nagging that might be holding you back, or you can use the exercise to help you deal with your Fearful Child that might be concerned about the future. You also get to send yourself some words of wisdom from the future to help you in the present moment.

Here are a few examples of how my clients and I have used this process:

- A friend who was about to go off and do VSO explored the future in terms of two possible locations that she might end up in.
- A client walked into two different futures to explore two different career possibilities.
- A client who was getting married in the same week as she was moving house stepped into the future to work out how she could remain sane and make sure everything happened when it needed to.
- When working on multiple projects I used it to work out how they could be managed in a healthy and positive way.

Walking into the future exercise

Find a private place to do this exercise. You will need to walk along an imaginary line – so you might need to clear some space.

Step 1

Imagine a line that goes from your past to the future and decide which direction it is going in. Step on it in the present moment.

Step 2

Stand in the present, look at the future and think about whatever it is that you are exploring and just check in with your current thoughts and feelings about the future.

Step 3
Think about how far you want to walk into the future: a week, six months, a year, ten years, 30 years – whatever is appropriate for what you are exploring. Then walk along the timeline until you have got to that time in the future. Once you are there turn around and face where you have come from.

Step 4
Think about where you have got to, what you have achieved, how it feels, looks and sounds to be there in the future. Then look back over your timeline and the period of time it took to get here and think about:

- The key steps or milestones on your journey.
- Any obstacles encountered and how you overcame them.
- What supports and advisors you had along the way.
- What key lessons you have learned along the way.

Step 5
Now look back to where you started, imagine yourself back there. Think about what words of wisdom you want to give yourself to help you on your journey. Say these out loud to the 'you' who is back along the timeline in the present day.

Step 6
Now walk back along the timeline to the current time. Stand in the present time and take on board the words of wisdom from yourself in the future. Breathe deeply and take them on board. It helps to look up and visualise yourself living these wise words. See, hear and feel how great it is to be living these wonderful words of wisdom.

Step 7 (optional)
You can anchor these wise words by using 'Seven steps to anchoring resourcefulness', Part 4.

Getting reassurance from the future

When I was in the process of writing this book, I woke one morning feeling less than confident about myself and my little world. So I decided to visualise myself taking a walk into the future, exactly a year ahead to the following February. Once there, I stood and looked back on the year. I saw all the voluntary work I had done on an exhibition I was involved in, alongside all the workshops and consultancy that I had completed. From this future viewpoint, I passed words of wisdom back to myself, saying that, despite all the negativity that I was feeling each day, I was taking steps forward in terms of finishing my book, marketing my business and creating a great life for myself. I was able to reassure myself that at some point in the year a 'tipping point' was reached where everything fell into place. I felt quite emotional, in a good way, standing there in the future. When I moved back through time to the present I felt tearful, knowing that although it would be tough I would make it, I would succeed.

Malcolm Gladwell's idea of the 'tipping point' came to me through the exercise and was not one I had associated with my current situation. And I found it very reassuring to consider the year ahead in that way.

So if you feel overwhelmed by your current situation, perhaps despairing of ever moving forward, walk into the future to get a long-term perspective on your current situation. And you can gain some words of wisdom from the 'future you'.

The end of the inner critic

You might be asking 'Is it possible to totally stop or bring an end to the inner critic?' From my experience the inner critic is now silent about 90 per cent of the time. And when it does rear its ugly head I can spot it very quickly and take action to counteract it. So most of the time its impact is minimal or non-existent.

It might be possible for some people who have a less severe example of an inner critic to dispel it completely – and if you do I would like to hear from you!

Benefits of a life free from inner criticism

The benefits of being able to spend most of your time and life free from inner criticism are:

- Increased contentment and satisfaction with life and what you do.
- A more happy and positive attitude, even when faced with challenging times or situations.
- More creativity both in and out of work.
- Increased wisdom as a result of listening to your inner wisdom rather than your inner critic, thereby making wiser decisions.
- Improved ability to evaluate your work and performance to realistically see what you achieve and what you need to change.
- Ability to celebrate your successes and the journey you are on.
- Ability to spot when the inner critic kicks in and take action.

Inner wisdom

One of the biggest benefits you will gain from mastering your inner critic is getting in touch with your inner wisdom. As time goes on this will get stronger and stronger and easier to access. This wisdom will help you when you are feeling down and frustrated with life, when you need to make decisions and tackle problems. I believe that when our inner critic is out of control it is hard to hear our wise self – it gets shouted down and lost. Finding your inner wisdom is likely to have a huge positive impact on many areas of your life.

Freedom from your inner critic: what will your life be like?

Sit back for a moment and visualise what life will be like for you when you are free from the tyranny of your inner critic. See, hear and feel the difference. Perhaps picture yourself in situations where your inner critic might have taken hold of you and ask yourself:

Q. What does it feel like to feel positive about myself, and my life?

Q. How do I sound when I am in this positive state of mind?

Q. How do other people sound?

Q. How am I behaving when I am in this state? How do others react and behave towards me?

Q. What do I look like? What do I notice around me, that in the past I have failed to see?

When I am in a positive state of mind and free from the inner critic I feel taller, more expansive, I move around more freely, my voice sounds stronger and centred and I laugh more freely. I notice the good things around me, I see others who are happy. I notice the beauty of nature, even if I am in the middle of a city or the weather is awful. I am also more compassionate and tolerant towards myself and other people, even when things do not go as planned.

Wouldn't it be great if we all felt like this? Not only would we feel better, but this would also be reflected in our environments and rub off on people we come into contact with in a positive way.

Practise, persevere and be patient

There is a wonderful quote from the thirteenth-century Buddhist priest Nichiren Daishonin that I often return to and it helps me to keep going in whatever I am attempting to achieve:

'The journey from Kamakura to Kyoto takes twelve days. If you travel for eleven but stop with only one day remaining, how can you admire the moon over the capital?'

He was talking about a journey of faith, and here we are talking about a journey of transforming a habit of a lifetime. Like any journey it is important to continue until you have achieved your goal so that you can enjoy the benefits when you get there. And like any journey it is important to enjoy the journey along the way, rather than wait until you reach your destination.

By using the techniques in this book, practising them with patience and perseverance, you will win through and get to admire the wonders in your life. I have absolute confidence from my experience that if you continue with this journey you will reach a state where you have 'mastered your inner critic' and gain all the benefits this brings.

Thank You to...

Tony Morris, my book agent, who on receiving my newsletter asked me if I had ever thought about writing a book, which was just what I was doing. His perseverance and support secured me a publisher.

Ali Cocks for her amazing friendship and support over the years and for reading, editing and giving me constructive feedback and encouragement on the first draft of this book.

Diane Mattinson who also thoroughly read the first draft and gave some very valuable feedback.

Stevie Knight for her brilliant cartoons and for bringing my words to life.

Jennifer Barclay from Summersdale for her trust and support in getting this book published.

Lucy York, my editor, for providing a different perspective on my book, enabling it to be a much better read in the end.

Breda Flaherty who has been an amazing Support and Challenge Partner over the years and spurred on my professional and personal development.

My dad who proofreads my monthly newsletter, which has helped me to enhance my writing skills.

My mum for our mutual love of art and all things creative.

My wonderful Sir Charles Napier colleagues who have sustained me over the years with very long lunches – you know who you are!

Inspirational Resources

Books

The following are just a few of the books that have inspired me over the years.

Angelou, Maya *Wouldn't Take Nothing for My Journey Now* (1993, Virago Press)
I started reading Maya's autobiography when I was made redundant in 1991 and found it so inspiring. This book contains bite-size morsels of her pearls of wisdom.

Dickson, Anne *A Book of Your Own* (1994, Quartet Books)
Anne has written so many wonderful books over the years. This provides daily inspiration and food for thought.

Dyer, Dr Wayne W. *Staying on the Path* (1995, Hay House Inc.)
I found this by chance and it opened up the world of Wayne Dyer to me. I dip into it when I need sustenance on my journey in life.

Dyer, Dr Wayne W. *The Power of Intention* (2004, Hay House Inc.)
Wayne is a truly inspirational writer, someone who writes from his heart and from his wealth of experience.

Ikeda, Daisaku *A Piece of Mirror and Other Essays* (2004, Soka Gakkai)
I've quoted Daisaku Ikeda in this book. He has written numerous books and speeches, but this small book provides inspiration on various topics from youth, ageing and marriage to war and peace.

Karsten, Peter *Be Great, Be You* (1999, Peter Karsten)
This little book produced by Peter, along with his cards, provides thought-provoking moments as you flick through it.

Kübler-Ross, Elisabeth and Kessler, David *Life Lessons – How Our Mortality Can Teach us About Life and Living* (2000, Simon & Schuster)
Having read most of Elisabeth Kübler-Ross's books over the years, this is the one I dip back into time and again. An amazing book that really makes you stop and think about your life.

Kundtz, David *Stopping – How to be Still When You Have to Keep Going* (1999, Newleaf)
Another book I often dip into. A great antidote to our inner critic that tells us we have to keep going no matter what. David shares his own and his clients' stories of using stillpoints, stopovers and grinding halts to take stock of and transform their lives.

McMillen, Kim and McMillen, Alison *When I Loved Myself Enough* (1996, Pan Macmillian)
I came across this and started reading it in a bookshop in Wellington, New Zealand. A chill ran down my spine as I read Alison's story about her mum's book. If there was ever a message to get yourself sorted and enjoy life now, this is it.

Neill, Michael *You Can Have What You Want* (2006, Hay House)
I've been subscribing to Michael's weekly coaching tips since the early 1990s, so when his book came out I had to get it. He writes from his own experiences and those of his clients, in a very practical and inspirational way.

Ryan, M. J. *The Power of Patience* (2004, Bantam Books)
This is a book I bought for my dad and then realised I needed! If you need to develop your patience then this book will assist you on your journey.

SARK *Living Juicy – Daily Morsels for Your Creative Soul* (1994, Celestial Art)
It was in about 1989 in Canada when I bought this and discovered the wonderful world of SARK. I have most of her books and recommend them all. This one provides some daily guidance in her own unique style.

Websites

www.grovelands.org.uk
To find out more about the consultancy services and training programmes that provide on management development, team working, communication and personal development then visit my website. You can also download free information sheets on various topics, and sign up for my free monthly e-mail coaching newsletter, Inspire.

www.artbystevieknight.com
Stevie Knight's inspiring cartoons appear in this book, She can create cartoons for use in presentations, training manuals, newsletters and company literature.

www.nlpu.com
If you want to find out more about NLP and Robert Dilts' seminars then take a look at the NLP University website. It has an encyclopaedia of NLP terms that is very useful.

www.sgi-uk.org and www.sgi-usa.org
To find out more about Nichiren Daishonin's Buddhism: the philosophy and practice, as well as events that are held around the UK and USA.

www.geniuscatalyst.com
Michael Neill has a weekly coaching newsletter which I use on a regular basis to boost my own self development.

www.planetsark.com
If you want to find out more about SARK and her inspiring books then take a look at her website and find inspiration on fulfilling your dreams and getting published!

www.chelseacards.co.nz
Inspirational quotes and art by New Zealand artist and writer Peter Karsten.

www.summersdale.com